THE STONEBRIDGE RAILWAY
A Portrait of a Midland Branch Line

The Stonebridge Railway tells an unusual story. A story of ambition, greed, and double-crossing. It tells of Royal favours and a noble contribution to war-torn Britain. Here the reader will find records of disasters amidst tranquillity, humour amidst rivalry. This is not fiction. This is what really happened in those early days of the Railway Mania. Deep in the heart of Warwickshire a battle was being fought, and its outcome would shape our railways forever. The men who fought it were giants – George Stephenson, his son Robert, and many others. A little line, just 7 miles long, became the focus of national attention. And then it was gone. As quickly as it was built, so it disappeared. But not without trace. This book salutes a part of Warwickshire's heritage that has no parallel in railway history.

Best wishes

Roger Waring

THE STONEBRIDGE RAILWAY

A Portrait of a Midland Branch Line

by

Roger Waring

Brewin Books

First Published
by Brewin Books, Studley, Warwickshire, B80 7LG
in December 1994

ISBN 1 85858 045 5

British Library Cataloguing in Publication Data.
A Catalogue record for this book is available from the British Library

Typeset in New Century Schoolbook by Avon Dataset Ltd, Bidford on Avon, Warwickshire B50 4JH
and made and printed by The Alden Press, Osney Mead, Oxford

Contents

The Stonebridge Hotel in 1902. The point at which the railway was due to cross the Birmingham to Coventry turnpike road, and the reason for the title – 'The Stonebridge Railway'.

CHAPTER ONE

Lost Lines of Arden

Railways do not have to be big to be famous. The Stonebridge Railway was a small undertaking – a little over 7 miles in length – but in its heyday it caused consternation on a grand scale. It was arguably *the* reason for the formation of one of the greatest railway companies of the nineteenth-century – "The Midland." Its beginnings had all the intrigues and cut-throat rivalry of a modern-day television drama. Its strategic importance and subsequent method of operation gave rise to bitter dispute, requiring the intervention of the Attorney General. The young Queen Victoria graced it with her presence and she was not the only monarch to appreciate its practical value. Wartime too, reserved for it a vital role. Its proponents included some giants of their age – George and Robert Stephenson, and Sir Robert Peel. Its supporters included a name synonymous with Warwickshire – Dugdale. Built to join the picturesque villages of Hampton-in-Arden and Whitacre, the line meandered peacefully through the water meadows of the neighbouring River Blythe, and in doing so traversed some of the prettiest parts of Warwickshire.

Behind this scene of apparent tranquillity, however, lay unremitting conflict, and in all too brief a time the route was to become an early casualty of nineteenth-century market forces. Such then, is the fame and the notoriety that attended the Stonebridge Railway. Despite its premature demise the line has a standing unique in the annals of railway history, and this account is dedicated to the preservation of its rich heritage. As such it does not pretend to be a treatise on the Midland Railway, about which much has already been written, and by authors better qualified that this one. Neither is it a formal history. Nevertheless, care has been taken to ensure accuracy in the telling of the story.

The building of the Stonebridge Railway recalls an age of high ambition, high ideals, and high risks; when pride in the job permeated the whole railway fraternity and service meant exactly that. Victorian influences came to dominate and despite the technical limitations of the age no efforts were spared in order to satisfy the expectations of the traveller – be he squire or labourer. Of course improvements did take time, and mistakes were made, but the Midland Railway was justly famous – it set standards that other companies had great difficulty in understanding, let alone equalling. Yet even in those heady days of constant mechanical innovation and thrilling engineering achievements, all journeys provided the opportunity for gentle observation of the passing country scene. It is hoped that the reader is provided with a flavour of those delights in the following pages.

Hampton Station.

CHAPTER TWO

Midland Beginnings

Early railway developments

Today, it is perhaps difficult for us to imagine the frenetic pace of activity during the 1830s and 1840s with regard to the formation of railway companies. The latter decade in particular came to be known as the era of "Railway Mania". Businessmen from every quarter were pouring money into a multitude of schemes – all designed to lure people and goods away from the overland coaches and canals. The novel alternative of faster more comfortable carriages hauled by steaming giants of the iron way was to prove irresistible. The number of Bills put before Parliament by 1845 had reached a staggering 1,428 – representing some £700,000,000 in capital investment. Amongst the very first of such schemes was the Grand Junction Railway – a line projected between Birmingham and the great conurbation of the North West of England. It opened in 1833 and five years later a connecting link was established between the two major centres of commerce in the British Empire – the capital of England and its second city. This was Robert Stephenson's monumental achievement – the London and Birmingham Railway. The prospect of establishing a lucrative network to support the movement of passengers and materials between the industrial heart of Britain and the metropolis became the over-riding consideration in the power struggles of the years that were to immediately follow.

The proprietors of the Stonebridge Railway were the Birmingham and Derby Junction Railway company and they are a principal subject of this account. Equally important to the account however are a number of other railway companies upon whose anticipated trade the Birmingham and Derby was almost totally dependent. Finally there is their chief competitor and opponents at law – the Midland Counties Railway. Let us therefore examine the respective credentials of the various concerns. It is necessary here, for the purposes of clarity, to anticipate events somewhat. This will help to explain the positions that the three main protagonists took, as they were not only all centred upon Derby, but were to be the constituent companies of that magnificent railway known as the "Midland".

The Companies

Firstly, we consider the senior partner in these affairs.

The North Midland Railway. (NMR) Royal Assent 4 July 1836

Formed to attract trade from the coal fields of the North Midlands and the North of England, this company had a colossus in their midst – George Stephenson. As consulting engineer to this, and other fledgling railways, his vision and energies were to transform transport in these Isles for all time. Having its Southern terminus at Derby, the company's line ran northwards via Rotherham to Leeds. The board of directors, as well as George Stephenson himself, were fiercely protective of their interests and are suggested by some as being the proximate cause of much of the subsequent conflict that was to embroil the competing companies.

Next, we assess the rivals.

The Birmingham and Derby Junction Railway. (B&DJR) Royal Assent 19 May 1836

The proprietors of this company included many well-known personalities. Sir Oswald Mosley Bart.; a landowner of Burton-on-Trent. Henry Smith; a Birmingham manufacturer of high social standing and first chairman of the board of directors. Abel Peyton; also of Birmingham, and subsequently deputy chairman. William Beale; one of the most respected inhabitants of Birmingham.

Samuel Beale; William's son. He later succeeded Henry Smith as chairman, and went on to hold that office within the Midland Railway. Daniel Ledsam; of Birmingham. Josiah Lewis; of Derby. Robert John Peel; Member of Parliament for Tamworth. They and numerous others were empowered to raise £630,000 in shares of £100. Together with those who gave direct financial backing to the scheme, there were many members of the landed gentry who considered that their interests would best be served by co-operating in the development of the railways. Three such prominent landowners were the Marquis of Anglesey; Sir Eardley Wilmot; and W.S. Dugdale.

Among the first officers appointed by the company were two whose names were to become synonymous with the Midland Railway; James Allport and Matthew Kirtley. Allport, first station-clerk at Hampton, went on to occupy the highest administrative positions in the railway world. Kirtley, locomotive foreman at Hampton, would in later life achieve universal and lasting fame.

The company was incorporated to provide Derby, and thence the North East, with a link to Birmingham and the South West. By connecting to the North Midland, and Birmingham and Gloucester Railways, this line would greatly accelerate the movement of raw materials and manufactured goods between the Midlands and the thriving ports of the Severn and Humber estuaries. In addition it would allow for the rapid and convenient transfer of passengers between the major centres of population. As exciting as this venture appeared, it did not arouse Derby folk. A public meeting arranged there to promote this great enterprise attracted a mere 12 inhabitants. Despite this apathy, plans proceeded apace.

George Stephenson was at the heart of matters in every respect, surveying the routes for his beloved North Midland as well as the Birmingham company. The North Midland line was expected to be a principal supplier of traffic to the Birmingham and Derby company. His son Robert had built the London and Birmingham line and so it can be seen that there was much of common interest at stake. The board of directors forged close links with the Stephensons in the prosecution of their joint ambitions – not only to complete the line as planned – but to serve the capital and its environs.

The original Birmingham and Derby proposals, prepared in the second half of 1834, identified principal stations at the two named towns, and the revenue estimates only took account of the anticipated North East to South West traffic. It was immediately evident, however, that by investing in a short additional spur from Whitacre to Hampton-in-Arden (near to Stone Bridge), the distance from Derby to London would be considerably shorter than if measured via Birmingham. Most important of all, the company could – at least in theory anyway – procure significant secondary income from the London traffic in return for the very modest outlay of £100,000.

Other stations proposed on this branch were at Coleshill and Whitacre, the latter being sited at the junction of the branch and the Birmingham line. It is this branch – the erstwhile "Stonebridge Railway" – that became the contentious issue, and also led to "Junction" being appended to the parent company's name.

The Midland Counties Railway. (MCR) Royal Assent 21 June 1836

The Midland Counties Railway Company initially linked Derby with Nottingham before embarking upon its main venture, which was to establish the more direct connection between the North and London. Its network of lines, surveyed by Charles Blacker Vignoles, used a south easterly exit from Derby to a point midway between that town and Nottingham, at Canfleet (close to Long Eaton). Here it turned southwards to Leicester and then Rugby, where it was planned to form a junction with the London and Birmingham line. Clearly this line would be a rival of the Birmingham and Derby Junction's for the through London traffic. The Midland Counties company not unreasonably regarded itself as the rightful carrier of this traffic, and in this respect it strongly resented the competitive aspirations of its neighbours.

Differences of opinion were not restricted to these two companies, however. In a similarly expansionist vein, the Midland Counties also had a deep desire to extend its influence to the area of country north of Derby. This was strictly Stephenson territory, and difficulties therefore arose in relationships with the North Midland Railway. The plan was to drive a line from the junction at Canfleet northwards towards Pinxton, there making a junction with the Mansfield to Pinxton railway. Further, it was hoped to eventually extend the line to Clay Cross as a means of forming a gateway to Sheffield. This route, if ever completed, would bypass Derby in the process. The townsfolk of Derby, as well as the directors of the North Midland, feared a resultant abstraction of through traffic if this line were to be allowed.

Although the initial part of it was justifiable, the implications for its onward development towards the North Midland's route were unmistakable. However, it is difficult to avoid the conclusion that the greatest objections arose because the extension *pointed North,* and as such clearly came into conflict with Stephenson's line. It is possible that the North Midland company actually prevailed upon the Birmingham and Derby to pursue the Stonebridge branch in direct response to this developing threat.

Finally, and briefly, we observe the bystanders.

The Birmingham and Gloucester Railway. (B&GR) Royal Assent 22 April 1836

This was the company upon whose traffic the Birmingham and Derby Junction relied most to justify its existence. The provision of a through route to the south-west gave access to the exporting centres vital to the Birmingham and Derby Junction's projected financial success. The eventual opening of this line a year and a half after their own must have been a source of some embarrassment to them.

The London and Birmingham Railway. (L&B) Royal Assent 6 May 1833

Officially this company was a disinterested party in the disputes that arose in later years between the two warring companies referred to, but in practice it was to make life quite difficult for the Birmingham and Derby Junction in a number of operational areas. Its main concern was for profits and in this respect it was undoubtedly successful. The construction of its line was a staggering feat, engineering on so vast a scale as to later invite comparison with the building of the Pyramids. Its successful completion brought Robert Stephenson universal fame.

Compromise and Double Dealing

We have seen from the foregoing how the two competitive schemes were evolving and the ambitions of each company. Conflict was by this time a real possibility. Prior to this, however, and particularly in the early days, the separate boards of directors were on reasonably amicable terms. They would discuss the relative merits of one another's schemes in a spirit of co-operation, as long as their own aspirations were undiminished. They were prepared to compromise where absolutely necessary. In an effort to resolve the growing differences that arose from the contentious proposals, discussions had been held at Derby in December 1835. These talks involved not only the representatives of the respective railway companies, but also MPs and civic dignitaries from the towns affected. The result was an agreement – that both the Clay Cross extension and the Stonebridge branch would be withdrawn from the bills to be submitted to parliament. Had all sides honoured this treaty to its full extent there would be no story to tell, but from 1836 onwards matters became decidedly Machiavellian in nature.

The Midland Counties Railway company was evidently reluctant to relinquish its options on this northern route. At the last possible moment the directors made an application to parliament

for appropriate powers. That this deviousness was not expected by the directors of the Birmingham and Derby company is perhaps to their credit, but their counterparts at the Midland Counties had in earlier years already demonstrated their capacity for concealment, if not blatant deceit. During 1833 they had been obliged to advertise in the local press the proposed route of their line and its junction at Rugby. They chose for these notices the most obscure newspapers imaginable. Not until early in 1836 did the inhabitants of Northampton realise the truth of the matter – that their town was not to be on the main line. Realising the seriousness of the omission they became desperate to secure main line access. Hurried proposals for a competing line were promoted, and in the ensuing wrangling a clause was inserted into the Midland Counties bill that prevented the early construction of the intended section from Leicester to Rugby. In the meantime an alternative site at Roade was considered for the junction with the largely fanciful South Midland Counties Railway. Although the scheme failed this procrastination was to critically hinder progress of works on the Midland Counties railway.

In 1838 too, the Midland Counties directors were to strike a secret deal with the North Midland Railway on division of traffic. For their part the directors of the Birmingham and Derby Junction considered matters settled as a result of the 1835 agreement with the Midland Counties, and they removed the Stonebridge branch from their own bill. When they subsequently became aware of advertisements for the Midland Counties' disputed extension their response was immediate and effective. A separate act was prepared for the formation of "The Stonebridge Junction Railway Company." Its surveyed route coincided exactly with the line of the original branch. The directors hoped that their two bills might be combined during their passage through parliament. In this respect they were wholly successful.

The directors of this company were not idle or unambitious. They were astute businessmen who had anticipated the competition from, if not the ruthlessness of, the Midland Counties Railway company. It must be admitted that nevertheless, they were equally responsible for the conflict. The basis on which their company had been formed was to build a railway intended *entirely for other purposes*. The proposal to build a competitive line was therefore clearly in breach of parliamentary guidelines. Therein lies the rub. With the support of Sir Robert Peel – Member of Parliament for Tamworth, and later to become Prime Minister – it is hardly surprising that any initial objections were overcome. Further

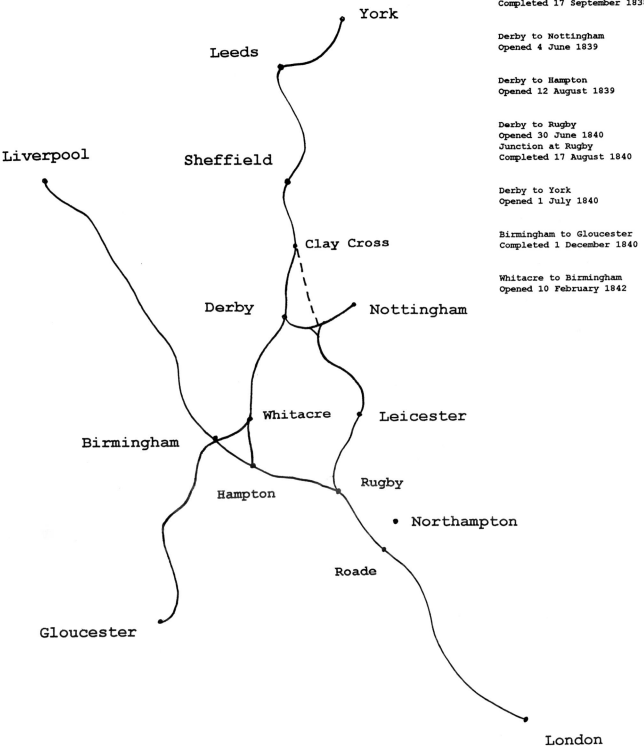

York

Leeds

Liverpool

Sheffield

Clay Cross

Derby

Nottingham

Whitacre

Leicester

Birmingham

Hampton

Rugby

Northampton

Roade

Gloucester

London

Birmingham to Liverpool
Completed 4 July 1837

Birmingham to London
Completed 17 September 1838

Derby to Nottingham
Opened 4 June 1839

Derby to Hampton
Opened 12 August 1839

Derby to Rugby
Opened 30 June 1840
Junction at Rugby
Completed 17 August 1840

Derby to York
Opened 1 July 1840

Birmingham to Gloucester
Completed 1 December 1840

Whitacre to Birmingham
Opened 10 February 1842

——————— Lines built

- - - - - - Lines proposed

Map of network in 1842.

examples of their ambitions are appropriate.

At about the same time that they were conceding the Stonebridge branch early in 1836, the directors foresaw the need for a line along the Trent Valley from Manchester that would provide an even more direct route to London than that via Birmingham, or for that matter, Derby. The Manchester South Union Company proposed a line to reach Tamworth at which point it would meet the Birmingham and Derby Junction's own tracks. Perhaps in response to the concession of the Stonebridge branch the directors of the Birmingham and Derby Junction decided to examine more urgently ways by which they could compensate for its loss. Plans were accordingly submitted to Parliament on their behalf detailing the construction of a line from Tamworth to Rugby. The scheme provoked a hostile response from the London and Birmingham, Grand Junction, and Midland Counties Railway companies, as well as objections from numerous influential landowners. Whilst this opposition was perhaps not wholly unexpected, powerful pressures were clearly brought to bear during the bill's passage through the Commons. A single barn had seemingly been left out from the surveyor's map, and this omission – of a very trifling nature – was deemed sufficient grounds upon which to ensure the failure of the bill on a technicality. The loss of this line was an unexpected and bitter blow to the company, and they tried to obtain recompense accordingly. In this respect they were unremitting, but unsuccessful.

Had this line gone ahead the Stonebridge branch would have been sacrificed regardless of other events. It is even possible that the Birmingham and Derby route itself might have been abandoned. Plans were also prepared in later years for connections from Hampton to Ashchurch (near to Tewkesbury) thereby avoiding the Lickey incline; and Banbury via Barston and Knowle, thus anticipating the GWR line. This latter proposed line had a spur to the canal wharf at Catherine-de-Barnes. Had these plans come to fruition Hampton might well have grown into a sizeable town rather than remain a village. Its population was 3306 in 1841. Solihull's was 3401. How easily their fortunes could have been reversed!

The battle for domination

Initially the North Midland took a benign view of the routes planned in 1834 by the Birmingham and Derby Junction, mainly as a result of Stephenson's influence in both camps. Subsequently however, the directors of the North Midland were not always so open in their dealings with the Birmingham and Derby Junction. On 30 March 1838 – well before any of the Derby based lines were opened – the arrangements for working through trains were the subject of a restrictive agreement between the North Midland and Midland Counties to the certain detriment of the Birmingham and Derby Junction. Born out of desperate compromise this agreement was a sop to the Midland Counties for the relinquishment of their Clay Cross extension. The conditions were to the effect that upon the eventual opening of the Derby to Rugby line the North Midland would send its through traffic by this route, rather than via the longer distance of the Birmingham and Derby Junction's. It was to run for a period of 7 years. The exposure of this agreement in later years was to sour relations among all three parties and the interpretation of it gave rise to a crippling rate war.

Whilst the aim of all of the companies concerned was to open their routes to traffic at more or less the same time in order to obtain common benefits, there was understandably more urgency to complete works that linked to lines that were already in use by this date. By 1838 the London and Birmingham and Grand Junction Railways were carrying traffic, so for this reason the Birmingham and Derby Junction was especially motivated to pursue its cause with the maximum energy. This was reinforced due to its rival, the Midland Counties, having to delay construction work on the Leicester to Rugby section until the summer of 1837. As the works here were expected to be especially heavy it was an obvious and serious disadvantage.

This then was the scene that presented itself to the Birmingham and Derby Junction directors in the Spring of 1837: Their attempts to build a line from Tamworth to Rugby had been thwarted despite determined efforts. The connecting line to Gloucester was unlikely to be opened in the immediate future. They had the means to build speedily from Derby towards Birmingham. They had the necessary legislation to construct a cheap, short, double track branch to Hampton that would give them access to the London and Birmingham line – a track that would require no significant feats of engineering. Their opponents were hampered by obstructive legislation. If it could complete the whole route from Derby to Hampton before the Midland Counties opened the competitive line, the Birmingham and Derby Company would obtain an early monopoly on the through London traffic. This monopoly could well prove decisive.

It is little wonder that the directors decided as they did. They went for Hampton. Not only that, they temporarily abandoned Birmingham, leaving the direct connection in abeyance for another 5 years. This act was a considerable breach of faith towards the citizens of that town and as such did not commend itself to those who later had to sit in judgement on the company. It made railway history, though.

Robert Stephenson. Engineer-in-chief of the B&DJR.
National Railway Museum

George Stephenson. He carried out the initial surveys for the B&DJR in 1836.

National Railway Museum

Charles Blacker Vignoles. Engineer in charge of the rival Midland Counties Railway.
National Railway Museum

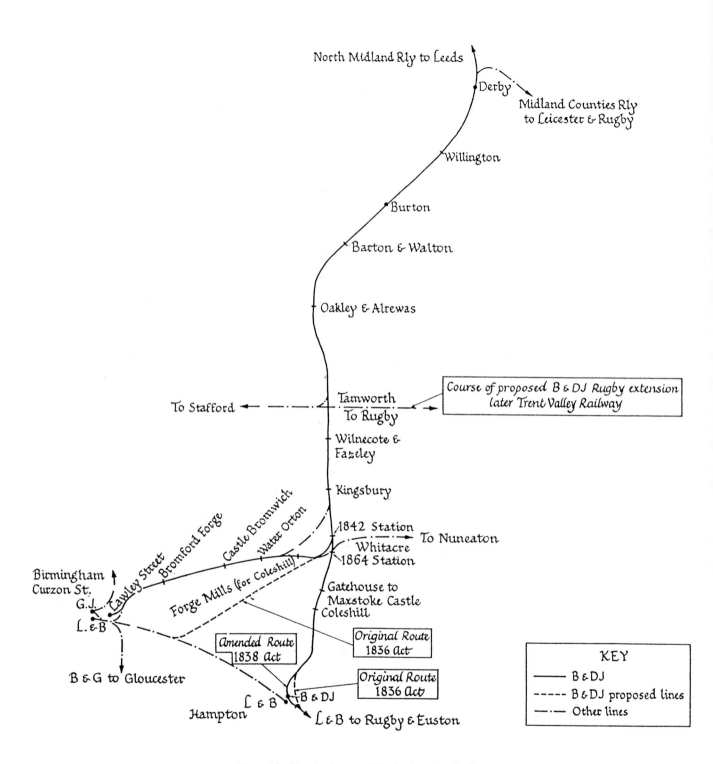

Map of the Birmingham and Derby Junction Railway

CHAPTER THREE

The Making of the Stonebridge Railway

Construction

George Stephenson surveyed the company's lines in 1834 and 1835, assisted by William Fowler. Basing his operations at the Hen and Chickens public house in Birmingham, he was frequently to be seen out and about on his yellow post-chaise. By the middle of 1835 he was able to report that there were no problems with the proposed route to Birmingham. The one chosen largely followed low-lying areas, and the works were therefore expected to be light. The distance between the major towns was 38 1/2 miles. It was intended to join with the London and Birmingham's line at Stechford as well as at Hampton. This plan was postponed following the decision to complete a double track line from Derby to Hampton as quickly as possible. On 22 September 1836, at the first public meeting of the proprietors, George Stephenson was entrusted with full responsibility for the line. Due to his commitments with the North Midland he recommended that the Birmingham and Derby Junction allow his son Robert to take charge as Engineer-in-Chief. One can imagine that the appointment of the man who had masterminded the building of the London and Birmingham line was a welcome one. It must have added significantly to the prestige of the project. Robert Stephenson, in turn, assigned responsibility for construction work to John Cass Birkinshaw, also an engineer of high repute. As resident engineer his target date for completion was June 1839.

Contracts were let, of which the Whitacre to Hampton branch comprised two short sections; Maxstoke (3 1/4 miles); and Stonebridge (4 miles). General works on the whole line then commenced in August 1837. Initially concentrated at the Derby end, they had by the end of that year progressed as far as Tamworth. As the nature of the works was heavier here than on the Stonebridge section, it was always recognised that the southern half could be left until the end. It was not until 1838, therefore, that excavations started in earnest on the final 7 miles to Hampton. The branch was originally intended to pass close to Stone Bridge, on the Birmingham to Coventry turnpike road. It would then have carried across Diddington Lane to meet with the London and Birmingham's line along the course of Marsh Lane, near to a fourteenth-century packhorse bridge. The junction, had it been effected here, would have been on a long incline of 1:330. Before construction could be started on this section, however, an alteration was requested in 1838 in order to avoid Packington Park, the seat of the Earl of Aylesford. Why his Lordship did not object earlier is unclear, but he at least met the cost of the amending Act of Parliament. Its effect was to set the line further west by about a mile during its approach to Hampton. Charles Liddell surveyed this new portion on behalf of George Stephenson.

The contracts for the track, stations, and bridges between Kingsbury and Hampton had by this time already been let to W. & J. Simmons. Amongst the names of sub-contractors employed here were David McIntosh, J.T. and G. Leather, and John Waring. Simmons accordingly delayed commencement of work on the Stonebridge contract until the new legislation was enacted. In practice, the works on the deviation were considerably easier than those on the original line. The crossings of the turnpike roads were improved and the length of the whole reduced by some half a mile. The planned site for the junction station was moved nearer to Birmingham by a similar distance. This increased the distance to London by about a quarter of a mile overall, but as the gradients were considerably eased no journey time was expected to be lost as a result. On 27 July 1838 the amending act was passed, and work then commenced on the final section. The contractor had been active on the Maxstoke portion since April, making good progress.

A primary concern of the engineer was to arrange for cuttings and embankments to cancel each other out as far as possible. The composition of the soil in this part of Warwickshire was a mixture of marl, sand, and large amounts of gravel. The lie of the land on the surveyed route was such that virtually all of the material generated could be put to good purpose. On the Stonebridge contract there were 239,000 cubic yards to be excavated, of which 178,000 was used in forming embankments. The greater part of the remainder was laid upon the permanent way as ballast. The cutting at Bickenhill provided for the raised earthworks at Hampton, and the excavations in Siding Wood supplied much of the material used for the embankment that cut across Packington Park.

The original line crossed the small River Bourne near to Whitacre and the modest brick built bridge survives to this day. The larger River Blythe was crossed in six places, timber being used for five of the bridges. These five were all built on bends in the river, so erosion was minimised. A small iron girder bridge was built near to Dukes Bridge to span a dead arm of the Blythe following diversion of the main stream. On a straight stretch of water near to Castle Farm the bridge demanded more substantial works; and the timbers had supporting stone piers to afford extra protection against the faster current.

One other particular bridge deserves special mention. During the planning of the line, it was also necessary to divert the course of the river in Packington Park so as to avoid unnecessary expense. This resulted in the loss of an established estate bridge. By way of compensation the railway company agreed not only to provide a new one, but also to maintain it. The rather elaborate affair that resulted became something of an anachronism in later years. It was maintained by subsequent railway companies for over a century, right up to nationalisation in 1947.

The land overbridges were a mixture of brick and local sandstone. Of those surviving, a small sandstone viaduct in Packington Park is of unusually fine construction, having stone voussoirs and piers. Two similar, but smaller spans having skew arches are also very attractive. The brick built over bridges were generally elliptical in design; frequently crowned with stone parapets; and in some cases having stone quoins as a further decoration. The two bridges that carried turnpike roads over the line were necessarily more substantial. Although of a squarer form, they nevertheless made handsome use of the local stone. It is noticeable that all the bridges visible from within Packington Estate have an air of grandeur not found elsewhere.

Where small watercourses had to be channelled beneath the track then simple brick culverts were invariably built. Many of these culverts still perform adequately today, with little visible deterioration. Where level farmland was crossed that demanded access from both sides, ramps and gates were installed. In embankments, small under bridges were built consisting of longitudinal iron girders set into brick abutments.

To the track itself. The term *permanent way* is something of a contradiction. It was used simply to differentiate between the actual track to be laid and the *temporary way* that allowed access during construction of the railway. In practice, the permanent way is anything but, due to the ever-present needs for maintenance. As built here, it consisted of iron rails of the single parallel type, 57lb. per yard, set on kyanised larch sleepers laid in the transverse fashion at 3ft intervals. The Stephenson "narrow" gauge of four feet eight and a half inches was naturally used, with the lengths of track being connected by the usual fish plate method. The rails were positioned in iron chairs, and then secured by wooden keys (small blocks of oak) that were wedged into place. Prior to installation these keys were steamed, then greatly compressed, before being stored in the dry. Upon fitting and subsequent exposure to the moist atmosphere, they expanded to grip the rails in a most effective manner. Sometimes this expansion was so great as to rent asunder the iron casing. These forms of inside keys were to be found in use on the line at Hampton up to the very end.

The first rails and chairs were supplied by a Stourbridge firm, John Bradley and Co., at a cost of £11.10s and £8.10s per ton respectively. Subsequently, Foster and Co. of Birmingham successfully tendered at £9.15 and £7.10s per ton. Following completion of the initial operating period (during which time the main contractor was responsible for the state of the line) maintenance contracts were awarded. In July 1840 John Stephenson successfully tendered for the 14 1/2 mile section north of Hampton at a cost of £250 per mile, per annum, reducing to £240 and £190 in the two succeeding years.

The original branch had two stations – Hampton (first-class) and Coleshill (second-class) – plus various small crossing points. Hampton provided the connection with the prestigious London and Birmingham line, and was thus something of a showpiece. This single-storey building was similar in style to the toll-houses to be found on turnpike roads but unlike those it was used solely for company business. Having a striking bay window with inset stone piers, particularly fine brickwork, and unusual guttering, it had, and still has, a very pleasing appearance. In order to serve the Birmingham bound trains from London, a small platform was built on the opposite side of the London and Birmingham line, at the bottom of a small wood that formed part of Sir Frederick Peel's estate. A noted landowner, he became

Hampton Station c. 1875. The former 'Derby Junction' of 1839. The large island platform is clearly visible in this very old view. The canopy on the left is of LNWR origin, as is the engine of the local train. The locomotive to the right is a double-framed Kirtley 0-6-0.

Courtesy Dr. Alan Smyth

Coleshill station c.1906. William Leary poses for the camera. Beneath bridge 8 in the distance can be seen MP2 in its original position, and to the left of it part of the Coleshill distant signal post.

Warwick County Museum

Vale House – 1954. The shared home of James Allport and Matthew Kirtley.

P S Garland collection. Courtesy R S Carpenter

Maxstoke Lodge – March 1991. Virtually unchanged from 150 years ago.

R N Waring

The handsome skew arch bridge 8 at Coleshill c. 1963. The post of MP2 is adjacent to the bridge. Coleshill station was a few yards beyond it.

T H Messenger

Hampton locomotive shed a mere 40 years ago! The considerable size of the building is well shown here. Photo dated 20th May 1954.
Courtesy R S Carpenter

OPENING OF THE BIRMINGHAM AND DERBY JUNCTION RAILWAY.

—The Public is respectfully informed that on and after MONDAY, the 12th of AUGUST inst., the TRAINS of this Company will START from the Station of the London and Birmingham Railway, in BIRMINGHAM, and from the Company's Station in DERBY; and also that Passengers between London and Derby may be booked throughout as below mentioned :—

HOURS OF DEPARTURE.

FROM BIRMINGHAM.		FROM DERBY.	
H.	M.	H.	M.
7	30 morning.	7	0 morning.
1	0 afternoon.	11	30 ditto.
6	30 ditto.	4	30 afternoon.

SUNDAY TRAINS.

7	30 morning.	7	0 morning.
7	0 afternoon.	7	0 afternoon.

Coaches to Nottingham, Sheffield, Leeds, York, and all parts of the North, will leave Derby immediately on the arrival of each Train. | Coaches from Nottingham, Sheffield, Leeds, York, and all parts of the North, will arrive in Derby in time for each Train.

FARES.

	1st Class.	2d Class.	3d Class
Between Birmingham and Derby..	10s	7s	5s 0d
Between Hampton and Derby.....	8s	6s	4s 6d

DERBY TO LONDON.

Passengers may be booked through from Derby to London by the Trains leaving Derby, viz. :—

H.	M.	H.	M.
At 11	30 morning.	At 4	30 afternoon.

LONDON TO DERBY.

Passengers may be booked in London throughout to Derby, by the Trains leaving the Euston-square Station of the London and Birmingham Company, viz :—

H.	M.	H.	M.
At 8	45 morning	At 2	0 afternoon.

FARES.

	1st Class.	2d Class
Between London and Derby......	£1 15 0	£1 4 0

By order, THOMAS KELL, Secretary.

Birmingham, Aug. 3, 1839.

Facsimile of the official announcement of the opening of the railway

influential as a Railway Commissioner, and this enabled him to arrange for the London trains to call at Hampton in later years despite its modest status as a junction. An island platform was added to facilitate connecting services.

By comparison Coleshill (renamed Maxstoke in 1923), was a much more modest affair. It was built by William Mammatt in 1838/9 for £267. This two-storey house comprised the usual facilities for the travelling public, whilst also providing living accommodation for the station-master. His duties included acting as crossing-keeper for the gates on adjacent Maxstoke Lane. Sadly the station was demolished in 1962. Near to Blythe Hall, a separate crossing-keeper's house was built on the western approach to Maxstoke Castle. It has survived, and is of an ornate turreted design, very much in the style of the Fetherston-Dilke family's main residence.

The company built a two-road engine-shed for 4 locomotives at Hampton, of which only the west wall remains. Much of the shed was lost in a fire in 1977, but good photographic evidence survives to show off its original features. Nearby, a large detached two-storey building was erected to accommodate the company's officers. It became known as Vale House and, fortunately, it too has survived.

Grand opening

By February 1839 Birkinshaw was able to present a very satisfactory report. Nearly all the fencing was fixed in place, and the earthworks were almost finished. Most bridges had been built, with the ones over the River Blythe due for completion by April. The tracks were laid for just over half the distance between Hampton and Derby. With more than 2800 men employed on the whole route, he expected the line to be ready for use by July and, importantly, within the sum estimated at the beginning. There then followed heavy rains during the summer of 1839 and this delayed the opening by a few weeks.

His report of 26 August states ... "The stations at Burton and Hampton will be completed in the course of the ensuing month" ... "Eight Locomotive Engines have now been received and four are in the course of delivery" ... "A considerable number of Coaches have been placed upon the Line and in a few weeks more a stock of Carriages will be ready, sufficient for the requirements of every kind of traffic at present contemplated." On 29 May an examination of the whole route was made by special train, and on 15 July Robert Stephenson drove the six-wheeled Mather Dixon locomotive *Derby* from Birmingham to Derby and back. Two days later the Board of Trade inspector examined the works. The following is an extract

from the Directors' report to the proprietors' meeting of 29 August, on the state of the line. "The Directors cannot dismiss this part of the subject without stating their entire satisfaction with the manner in which the Works have been executed, and the unusual rapidity with which they have been urged forward." Birkinshaw had done his job well.

At the same meeting, the Directors outlined their proposals for an independent terminus at Lawley Street, Birmingham. The revised route would follow the Tame Valley, and the junction at Stechford would thus be abandoned. The sting in the tail of the report was ominous, however ... "It is evident, moreover, that the resources of the Line cannot fully appear until the North Midland Railway has been opened, and the Railway communication with Gloucester and the South is completed."

The line was formally opened on Monday 5 August 1839, one week before public services were due to start. It was a grand affair. A special train was provided, hauled by another Mather Dixon locomotive, *Tamworth*. The event was covered in great detail by the press. Some extracts from the *Railway Times* of the day provide the best means of describing the occasion. The reference to Blythe relates to the site of Coleshill station.

"On Monday last the Directors and a large party of Shareholders and their friends made an experimental trip along the whole of the line, previous to the opening of the railway, which takes place on Monday next. Ten o'clock having been fixed upon for starting, at this hour about a hundred and fifty gentlemen assembled at the London and Birmingham station, where a train of four first class and three third class open carriages, was in readiness for their accommodation. The carriages are similar in most respects to those already in use on the London and Birmingham and Grand Junction lines, the first class are very handsomely finished, the body of the carriages being painted a bright yellow, and the only external ornament which they bear is the arms of the company, which are elegantly emblazoned on the panel of the centre doors. Each carriage bears a number instead of a name, a practice which is now adopted on many of the railways recently opened. The second class carriages will, we understand, be enclosed, but none of them having been in readiness for the trip, we are unable to give any particulars as to their construction. All, however, who have travelled in cold or rainy weather in the second class carriages of the London and Birmingham line will be free to admit that the Directors have acted judiciously and liberally in adopting the improvement we have mentioned. The third class carriages are painted a dark brown, they are built in a very substantial manner, and each, it is calculated, will accommodate about forty persons. On the present occasion, from the extreme fineness of the day, and the anxiety evinced to obtain an uninterrupted view of the line and the country on either side, they were occupied by many gentlemen in preference to the first class carriages. The party having taken their seats, the train started from the London and Birmingham station about 20 minutes past ten, and proceeded at a rapid rate up the line as far as Hampton-in-Arden, a distance of nine miles, where the line to Derby commences. The junction is effected at this point by means of what are technically called switches, affording every facility for the trains from London or Birmingham passing up the Derby line. A commodious engine house is already built here, and a first class station is in the course of erection, which we believe, will be used by both Companies. Most of the works at this end of the line are still unfinished, but they are in a sufficient state of forwardness to afford all the necessary accommodation for working the line by the time fixed for its opening to the public. After remaining some time at Hampton, the train started on the Birmingham and Derby line at five minutes to eleven, amidst the cheers of the spectators, in which the party heartily joined. The railway is, at this point, on a level with the London and Birmingham line, from whence it runs nearly due north to Derby, the whole extent of the new line, from one extremity to the other, being 38 3/4 miles, or 47 3/4 from Birmingham to Derby, a distance which it is proposed to accomplish in two hours and a half, but when the arrangements are rendered more complete, it will probably not occupy even this length of time. The train proceeded towards the village of Blythe, passing, for about three miles, through the estate of Lord Aylesford, of which many very beautiful and picturesque views were afforded to the party in their progress. From Blythe, at which a station is to be erected, Coleshill is distant about one mile. At this place the party were joined by W.S.Dugdale, Esq., one of the members for the northern division of the county, whose seat, Blythe Hall, is situated at a short distance to the west of the line. At half-past eleven the train arrived at Kingsbury, which is also fixed upon as a station, from whence, after a brief stay, it again proceeded on its way, the line affording strikingly beautiful views of the country on either side. The train arrived at the temporary station erected to the south of the town of Derby, at ten minutes past two, amidst the cheers of a numerous assemblage of persons, who had been for some time awaiting its arrival. The site of the grand station for the Midland Counties, the North Midland, and the Birmingham and Derby

Railways lies to the south-east of the town, and will be used in common by the three companies. On arriving at the Derby station, omnibuses and carriages were in readiness to convey the party to the King's Head Hotel, where an elegant collation had been prepared by order of the Directors, to which the numerous guests sat down at about three o'clock."

With Henry Smith, Chairman of the Board of Directors, presiding, there then followed numerous speeches, and much mutual congratulating. His first toast was the health of "Mr George Stephenson." The great man's remarks are worthy of note. "Mr Stephenson, in rising to acknowledge the toast, regretted his inability to do it as he could wish, but they all knew he was an indifferent hand at making speeches. He could only say that he had been fighting for this part of his profession (that is, in carrying out the railway system in this country,) for thirty years, and they might all imagine the pride he felt in seeing another of his favourite projects brought to maturity. This was one of the links in the line of railway communication which would shortly pass from London to the north, and he spoke with great confidence when he asserted that it would form a portion of the great line into Scotland. He had examined the country in various directions, and he felt justified in saying that no other line could be got equal to that through Derby, passing along the North Midland, the York and North Midland, and the Great North of England, to Newcastle and thence along the coast to Edinburgh. He was quite aware that there was another line to the east of their own, but still Derby would receive the full benefit of the great chain of communication he had pointed out. He hoped the two companies would ultimately come to terms which would prove mutually beneficial, if not, he could tell them that the Birmingham and Derby Company were able to crush them. He did not wish it to come to this, but if it did he was ready to contend for it, and he was sure he should conquer." Strong words indeed! They must have subsequently raised a few hackles, perhaps even serious doubts, among the directors of the Midland Counties company.

The next toast was to George's son Robert. In his usual modest way he gave full credit to his able lieutenant, John Birkinshaw, and proffered congratulations accordingly. Henry Smith assured the meeting that this was *the* toast in which he felt the deepest interest that day. He was of the opinion that . . . "few engineers could have brought to the work more fertility of resources, soundness of judgement, greater zeal, or more untiring activity than that which had been displayed by that gentleman, combining with all these valuable qualities a courtesy of manner, and attention to the suggestions of the Directors, which, while they commanded their respect, had also won their esteem. Although he had come amongst them as a stranger, he assured him that wherever he went, or whatever might be his future situation in life, that he would leave behind him friends anxious to assist him, and who would ever feel the deepest interest in his welfare." He then concluded by proposing three times three the health of Mr. Birkinshaw. In reply ... "Mr Birkinshaw regretted that he could not express in adequate terms his feelings on the present occasion, for the kind manner in which his health had been proposed and received. He could only say, that whatever humble abilities he possessed he had devoted them to the work in which he had been engaged, that he had given every hour of his time to the carrying out and completion of this important railway."

Some idea of the esteem in which Birkinshaw was held can be shown by the fact that he stayed with the company until the completion of the direct line to Birmingham in 1842. After concluding thanks from the Mayor of Derby, the party returned to Birmingham, arriving there at about eight o'clock. On the following Monday, 12 August 1839, the line was opened for public use, and a link established with the north of England that was, for a short but glorious period, the only means of travelling from London to Derby and onward towards Scotland. For two local dignitaries, W.S. Dugdale and Captain R.N. Fetherston-Dilke, special permission was granted allowing them to stop trains *at will* along the route. Travelling arrangements were not all sweetness and light in these very early days, though. Dr. Granville, the holder of ticket No. 1 describes his experiences.

The first train

"I happened to be on the spot (at Derby) the day on which the line to London was first opened. As a matter of study and curiosity I determined on taking my departure by it for the capital. All Derby was in a bustle on that eventful morning ... I was first on the spot, and had ticket No. 1. Every director was present. Preliminary experiments had been made daily for a week and upwards, yet everything seemed in a state of confusion, everybody spoke or commanded, and when the carriages were brought up to the temporary platform it was found that some-

thing had to be done to the iron stop on one of those circular moving machines in the ground which serve to turn the vehicles. The operation was performed with bad and inefficient tools, and took some time to be completed. This was not very encouraging to me, who was silently watching every movement, and saw all the hesitation and whispering and going to and fro around us. When all was ready, it was found that there were but few persons who would proceed, and the train ended by being composed of three or four first-class carriages only, certainly very splendid and comfortable. With these we started for Stonebridge, a few miles north-west of Coventry, where we expected to be taken in tow by a train from Birmingham. But we were not quite ready when the train came into sight, and it whisked along, giving us the go-by and leaving us in the lurch. However, a locomotive with suitable fuel and water was soon procured and tacked on to our three or four solitary vehicles, which started on their venture at the risk of finding every impediment and none of the ordinary aids on the road, inasmuch as we were interlopers on the line, appearing for the first time upon it, and not in our right and pre-concerted time. The consciousness of this made my travelling companions in the same carriage and myself somewhat nervous, yet we could hardly help smiling, in the midst of our apprehensions, at the vacant and stupefied stare of the workmen we found on the road and our own line, who had just time to scamper off, and at the astonishment of some of the policemen who were seen running to take up their flags which they had not expected to be so soon called upon to wave again after the passing of the last Birmingham train, and above all at the gaze of wonder and curiosity of all the people employed at the different stations, upon beholding the arrival of a total stranger on their premises. We made our journey good, nevertheless, and I inwardly thanked my stars to find myself again upon my legs, passing under Hardwick's splendid arch at Euston Grove, where we arrived in seven hours from Derby, no great performance truly, nowadays, for a distance of 135 miles!"

On this somewhat optimistic note the Stonebridge Railway commenced operations, so now let us examine two of the individuals most closely associated with its development. They were to bring fame and notoriety in equal measure.

Sir James Joseph Allport, 1811–1892.
National Railway Museum

Matthew Kirtley, 1813–1873.
National Railway Museum

Matthew Kirtley and family at Litchurch Grange, Derby. Ann, his wife is at the window, with daughters Emily, standing, and Elizabeth, c.1868.

National Railway Museum

CHAPTER FOUR

Two famous personalities

Matthew Kirtley

Born in Tanfield, County Durham on 6 February 1813, Kirtley came from a railway family, and was to devote his life to the industry. Upon the opening of the London and Birmingham line in 1837, he was employed by that company as an engineman, and is authoritatively reputed to have driven the first main line train into Euston from Birmingham. The Stephensons certainly held him in high regard, and recommended him to the Birmingham and Derby company in 1839. He was appointed under Birkinshaw as locomotive foreman at Hampton in charge of 4 engines. He and his wife Ann shared Vale House with James Allport and his family. Despite his limited responsibilities, his abilities soon marked him out for advancement. In 1841 he was made up to Locomotive Superintendent.

In 1844, at the amalgamation, the Stephensons' influence again prevailed and Kirtley was selected as Locomotive Superintendent to serve the whole of the Midland Railway. His appointment was questioned by many on the grounds that other engineers, notably Josiah Kearsley of the Midland Counties, were more suited. The Birmingham company was also the smallest of the three concerns. Nevertheless, Kirtley went on to justify the considerable faith shown in him, and he was to command Derby works for the rest of his life until his death in 1873. During those glorious years he introduced standardisation of locomotive design, and acquired a deserved reputation for producing engines of unrivalled longevity. Indeed, one of his locomotives, despite its great age, has been preserved. He championed the use of safer six-wheeled engines as opposed to the early four-wheeled designs. Kirtley was a man of humble origins and, like his mentor George Stephenson, a thoroughly practical man whose success was based upon a deep understanding of all aspects concerned with the mechanical complexities of steam engines.

A critic styling himself "Veritas Vincit" was extremely harsh in his judgement of Kirtley, when writing in a popular railway journal of the day. Kirtley's style of locomotive management was seen to be less than perfect due to his lack of formal apprenticeship, but in practice the actions complained of were probably dictated more by financial considerations than by incompetence. In later years this criticism was considered unfair, even petty, and viewed from a century and a half later, the results of his talents simply cannot be denied. "Old Matt", as he was affectionately known, died on 24 May 1873 a much loved man. The railway folk of Derby erected a handsome granite obelisk in his memory in the Old Churchyard. It contains the following inscription – "The way of the just is uprightness. [ISAIAH xxvi.7.]"

James Allport

A native of Birmingham, James Joseph Allport was born on 27 February 1811. His father William, a prominent and successful gun maker to His Majesty's Board of Ordnance, had his business at 8 Whittall Street. He had been particularly active as a result of the Napoleonic Wars. James's mother, Phoebe was a milliner by trade. His early days were spent being educated in Belgium. Upon his father's death in 1823, James, although of tender years, assisted his mother with the family business. In 1832 he married Ann Gold, aged 26. Seeing great opportunities in the emerging railway industry, he therefore applied for the position of "Station Clerk" to the newly formed Birmingham and Derby Junction Railway, working under Birkinshaw. His experience was enough to secure an appointment at Hampton when the station opened in 1839. The census of 1841 shows him living in nearby Vale House with his wife and two daughters – Charlotte, aged 7, and Mary Louise, aged 4. He was young, ambitious, and possessed great breadth of mind. Big in stature as well, he made a good impression on his new employers.

During these formative years he became increasingly influential in the running of the railway. He was instrumental in starting the fierce competition on fares with the Midland Counties Company – the first rate war in railway history. In 1840 he was commended for his action following an accident upon the line at Whitacre. By 1842 he had shown enough promise to achieve promotion to Traffic Manager in Birmingham and Goods Superintendent at Derby. Rapid success followed, and although in 1844 the amalgamation of the three companies forming the Midland Railway left him without a post, the chairman George Hudson recognised his qualities. Hudson used him in 1845 to show that the "narrow gauge" railways were still capable of high speed. On the evening of Hudson's election as MP for Sunderland, Allport travelled from that town to London and back, returning with copies of "The Times" containing his account of the election and its result. The papers were in the hands of the townsfolk by 10.00 a.m., before the formal announcement of the poll! This remarkable feat was achieved by travelling at an average speed of more than 40 mph.

After holding important posts in other fledgling railway companies, he was subsequently appointed to the Midland Railway in 1853 as its General Manager. He then became responsible for the large scale expansion of the company's routes, and a tremendous increase in traffic. At about this time he moved to Littleover, in Derby. His daughter Mary married Edward Moore Needham, a superintendent of the company. The two families were close friends. His other children were Emily, Howard Aston, Charles James and Agnes Lydia.

During his distinguished career James Allport introduced many innovative and lasting reforms. In 1872 the Midland Railway pioneered third-class coaches on all passenger trains at a penny a mile. In 1875 cheaper travel, covered seats, and enclosed carriages were provided for the poorer classes by the simple expedient of breaking up all third-class carriages and using the second-class ones in their place. These actions horrified the competing railway companies, but when the success of his methods proved not only popular with the travelling public, but also financially very successful, they had no option but to follow suit.

He saw the advantage of Pullman Car travel for the wealthier classes, and initiated their use in this country. With equal consideration for third-class passengers he encouraged the development of the exceptionally comfortable Midland Clayton coach. He oversaw the construction of St Pancras station in 1868, but his most enduring legacy must surely be the Settle and Carlisle line, built in the 1870's under his leadership, when everyone, including shareholders and competitors, considered the project wildly ambitious – even impossible. His attention to detail was uncompromising, and his prowess in front of parliamentary committees became legendary.

Midland Class 2P Nº 602 at Belper in 1928, where Sir James Allport's grave overlooks the line.

Authors collection

20

In 1880, upon his retirement, he was presented with a cheque for £10,000 by the grateful shareholders of the Midland Railway, and made a director of the company. Somewhat belatedly, he was knighted in 1884 for his services to the nation. He was the greatest railway administrator of the nineteenth-century. His energies were seemingly limitless – an Associate Member of the Institute of Civil Engineers; a Justice of the Peace; a Lieutenant-Colonel in the Engineer and Railway Volunteer Staff Corps; he even helped found the Railway Clearing House. It has been said elsewhere that he did for railway passengers what Rowland Hill did in postal reform.

He died at St. Pancras station on 25 April 1892 following a short illness. His body was brought back to Derbyshire by special train and he was buried in the cemetery at Belper. His coffin was carried to the family vault on the steep hillside by six uniformed Midland Railway guards. As it was lowered into the grave a Midland express, including a Pullman car in its formation, rushed by on the old North Midland main line.

His own words provide the best epitaph. Towards the close of a long and active career he reflected ... "If there is one part of my public life on which I look back with more satisfaction that on anything else, it is with reference to the boon we conferred on third-class travellers. I have felt saddened to see third-class passengers shunted on to a siding in cold and bitter weather – a train containing amongst others many lightly-clad women and children – for the convenience of allowing the more comfortable and warmly-clad passengers to pass them. I have even known third-class trains to be shunted into a siding to allow express goods to pass. When the rich man travels, or if he lies in bed all day, his capital remains undiminished, and perhaps his income flows in all the same. But when the poor man travels, he has not only to pay his fare, but to sink his capital, for his time is his capital, and if he now consumes only five hours instead of ten in making a journey, he has saved five hours of time for useful labour – useful to himself, his family, and to society. And I think with even more pleasure of the comfort in travelling we have been able to confer on women and children".

Birmingham and Hampton-in-Arden can be proud of their association with such a noble personage; one who epitomised not only the industry, but also the integrity of the Victorian age.

Over the next forty years these two men were to become a driving force in a golden age of transport. The decades that followed saw them both rise to great heights. The whole of the railway world was to benefit.

The Late Sir James Joseph Allport

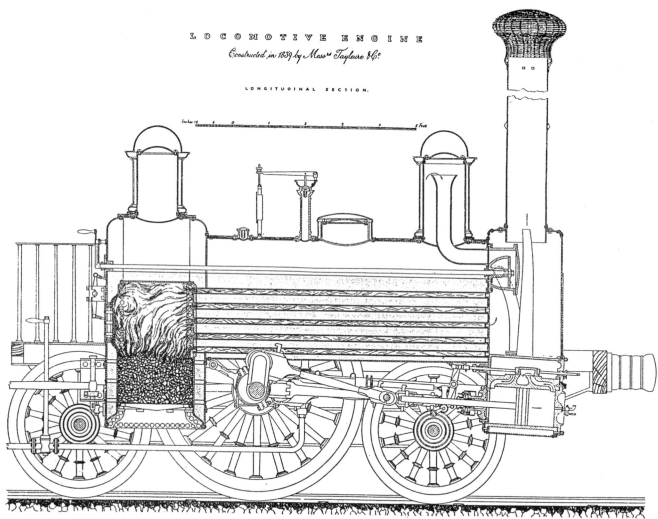

LOCOMOTIVE ENGINE

Constructed in 1839 by Messrs Tayleure & Co.

LONGITUDINAL SECTION.

REDRAWN·BY·OLAF·WILLIAM·BEWS·OF·FIBREGLASS·LIMITED·FROM·THE·ORIGINAL·BY·KIND·PERMISSION·OF·THE·VULCAN·FOUNDRY·LIMITED·OF·NEWTON·LE·WILLOWS·LANCASHIRE

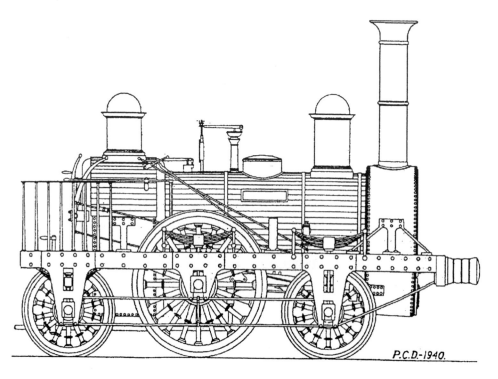

P.C.D.-1940.

Two drawings of Tayleur locomotives from 1839.

CHAPTER FIVE

The Glory Years 1839 – 1843

Locomotives and rolling stock

The company started operations with twelve locomotives; all of a six-wheeled design having a 2-2-2 arrangement. They were considered safer and more reliable than the four-wheeled engines in use on the London and Birmingham and Midland Counties railways. All engines were initially given names, and they were supplied as follows: From Mather, Dixon and Co., Liverpool, 3 engines named after villages – *Hampton, Barton,* and *Tamworth* delivered on 4 July 1839. From Tayleur and Co., Newton-le-Willows, 3 engines named after towns – *Derby, Birmingham,* and *Burton* delivered in July and August 1839. From Sharps and Co. 3 engines named after rivers – *Derwent, Trent,* and *Dove* delivered in the autumn of 1839. From R. & W. Hawthorn and Co., Newcastle, 3 engines also named after rivers – *Anker, Tame,* and *Blythe,* delivered in late 1839. In 1841 two further 0-4-2 engines for freight traffic were supplied by Thompson and Cole and were named *Kingsbury* and *Willington.*

The six-wheeled design was to cause early problems on the London and Birmingham line due to restricted turning facilities at Birmingham, and in September 1839 the Birmingham and Derby Junction company had their locomotive running powers rescinded between Hampton and Birmingham. Engines of the London and Birmingham company hauled their trains from that date.

Carriage design was simple, and based upon the horse drawn coaches of the day. All carriages had the company's very attractive armorial device emblazoned upon their centre doors. Although the term Coat-of-arms was used by many companies to describe their designs, only one company – the Great Central – actually applied for and were granted heraldic rights. The Birmingham and Derby's device enclosed the coats-of-arms of the two towns in a most attractive circular form. First-class carriages were bright yellow, seating 18 passengers; second-class blue, seating 24; and third-class dark brown, seating 40. All carriages were a little over 15 feet long and 5 feet high. Through carriages to and from London were

buff and black.

The company was progressive enough to provide enclosed second-class from the very beginning – a notable advantage over the rather basic coaches of other railway companies. Third-class, although open, at least had a roof. Some companies provided little better than cattle trucks for the cheapest form of travel. A first-class carriage made by Robert Jeffrey in 1840 cost £440 – a considerable sum. By contrast, Coleshill station cost £267 to build. The roots of the famous "Midland" standard of travelling comfort to come in the late nineteenth-century can thus be seen to date from these very early days. Wagons used for cattle and goods were of a very simple, but sturdy, four-wheeled design. Sideless, flat-bottomed trucks were provided for the conveyance of passengers' own horse drawn carriages.

Signalling

The signalling arrangements for the line were always minimal. The very early signals, points, and crossing gates were operated by railway policemen. Although in later years Coleshill and Hampton were provided with home and distant signals, and each had a signal "box", the line never had the standard block telegraph system installed throughout its length, and from opening to closure all trains were operated on a time interval basis. There was no communication between these two stations. This meant that the first knowledge that anyone at the stations had of any impending arrival was the engine's whistle and actual sight of the train.

Passenger services

In order to support the arrival of trains at Derby, an extensive network of connecting stage coaches was established for passengers wishing to travel onwards to such places as Sheffield, Leeds and York. The first train services comprised three a day each way between Derby and Birmingham on weekdays, with two each way on Sundays. Two of the

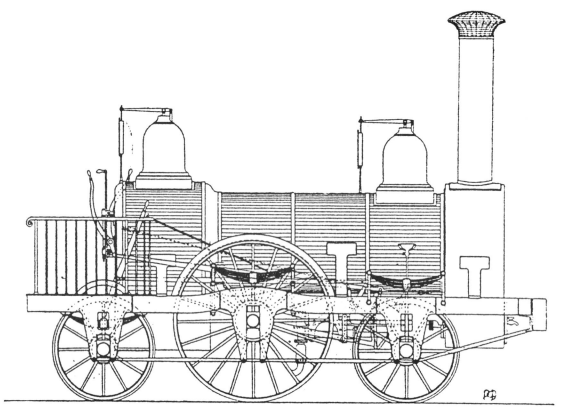

B. & D. J. R. Mather Dixon Single

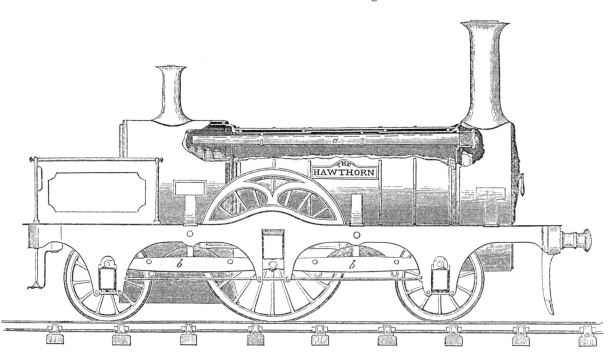

Hawthorn's Locomotive Engine.

B. & D. J. R. 2.2.2 loco Derwent *supplied by Sharp's, 1839.*

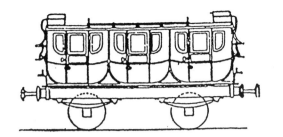 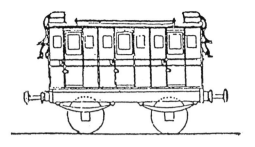

1st and 2nd class coaches, B. & D.J.R., 1839

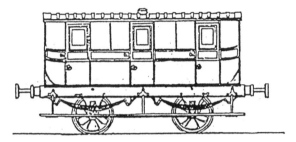

Midland Railway 3rd class coach.

Fares from Hampton. November 1840

	1st Class	2nd Class	3rd Class
Birmingham	3s 0d	2s 6d	2s 0d
Coleshill	1s 0d	0s 9d	0s 6d
Kingsbury	2s 0d	1s 6d	1s 0d
Tamworth	3s 0d	2s 0d	1s 6d
Barton & Walton	4s 6d	3s 6d	2s 6d
Burton	5s 0d	4s 0d	3s 0d
Derby	8s 0d	6s 0d	4s 6d
Coleshill to Whitacre 1842	1s 0d	0s 9d	0s 6d

weekday trains each way connected at Hampton for through services between Euston and Derby, with two coaches on each train being supplied for this purpose. The fastest journey between Birmingham and Derby was scheduled to take 2 hours. This included a necessary reversal at Hampton as the junction was laid facing towards London. This fact alone suggests the directors' true intentions in terms of potential sources of revenue. On 9 September 1839 a fourth daily train was added, together with an extra through coach.

By 1840 services had increased to five each way per day, including two night trains upon which the fares were slightly higher. An additional train ran on Sundays. For a brief period during that year the service reached six trains per weekday and four on Sundays, but the experiment was short-lived. For a full table of local fares at this time refer to page 25. The facsimile of the opening notice details the fares applicable to the main routes.

The rules of travelling etiquette were being established at this time, and very quickly a total ban on smoking was introduced. On 26 August 1839 a notice was issued forbidding smoking on the company's trains or in their stations. They had a problem with loiterers too – all officers were instructed to prevent individuals "hanging around" stations. By 1842 the facilities at Hampton were getting quite up-market – a full Justices Licence was granted allowing the sale of alcohol. This lasted for twenty-three years until 1865. The licensee was always named as that for *The Engine*, a nearby hostelry. The company had the fastest train on the narrow gauge too – the 10.50 a.m. passenger service from Hampton to Derby averaged 23.1 mph in 1841. Only Brunel's broad gauge engines performed better. By the end of the first two weeks of operation the railway had safely transported 7230 passengers.

Goods traffic

Very little freight was carried in the beginning. Letters, parcels, dogs, horses, and horse-drawn carriages were the main source of non-passenger business. The convenience of using the railway for transporting horses to distant hunts was immediately appreciated. They had to be at the station in good time though, initially 15 minutes prior to departure. Up to 1841 no agricultural produce was being carried, and few cattle. The problem was twofold – the Birmingham and Gloucester Railway was not yet open to generate badly needed traffic – and the postponed direct line to Birmingham was needed together with an independent terminus. Only then would the company acquire sufficient land to accommodate and expand its freight

operations. When Lawley Street goods station did finally open in 1842, traffic increased noticeably. The returns of 1843 list first-class goods such as coal, coke lime iron castings, and clay. Second-class goods included sugar, grain, earthenware, timber, metals, chains, and hardware. Third-class goods encompassed cottons, woollens, drugs, manufactured goods and general merchandise. It is difficult to say just how much of this was carried on the Stonebridge Railway in these very early days, but it is likely that coal was the main source of mineral revenue.

Accidents

Initially there were some minor problems – the Sharps engine *Dove* broke some iron rail chairs at Hampton, probably due to poor maintenance of the permanent way on the London to Birmingham line, and there were difficulties on the turntable at Birmingham. On 2 December 1840, however, a serious collision occurred at Whitacre. The 5.30 p.m. Hampton to Derby train hit an obstruction in the dark. The report in Aris' Birmingham Gazette is comprehensive:

"An inquest was held on Friday last and continued by adjournment on Saturday at The Swan Inn, Nether Whitacre before G.C. Greenway Esq., one of the Coroners for this county on the body of Richard Bluck, a labourer in the employ of the B&DJR, who was killed on the line near Whitacre in an accident during the progress of one of its trains on Wednesday evening last. The train came into contact with a small hand truck, or *lurry*, which two men King and Barber, employed by a contractor, were using improperly on the line. It was proved that they were warned twice to avoid the train to which the accident occurred, but notwithstanding this caution they continued to use the truck upon the line. The night being very dark, the driver was not able to perceive the obstruction, and his train ran over the truck, thereby throwing the engine and two of the third-class carriages off the rails. The deceased being in one of the carriages, was killed on the spot. The fireman was severely injured. The driver, thrown into an adjoining field, escaped unhurt. Another passenger, and B&DJR labourer, Naylor was also severely hurt. A female in another carriage received contusions to her shoulder but was able to proceed to Derby. It was proved by witnesses that the use of the truck violated company regulations. The jury returned a verdict of Manslaughter, and the two prisoners were committed for trial. The Coroner in his address said the B&DJR were free from blame but the contractor foreman was guilty of gross negligence. Fireman and Naylor recovering. Mr

The Engine Hotel c. 1930. The licensees named for Hampton Station from 1842–1865 were always the same as for this hotel.
Courtesy Mike Bryant

A platelayer's lurry.

BIRMINGHAM & DERBY JUNCTION RAILWAY.

Miles	DERBY TO BIRMINGHAM AND LONDON. STATIONS.	§ Mixed, 8 a.m.	§ 1st and 2d class carriages only, 11½ a.m.	§ 1st class with 2d class carriages 2¼ p.m.	§ Mixed, 4¼ p.m.	§ 1st class with 2d class carriages 9 p.m.	Sunday Trains. § Mixed, 8 a.m.	Mixed, 5½ p.m.	§ 1st class with 2d class car. 9 p.m.
		h. m.	h. m.	h. m.	h. m.	h. m.	h. m.	h. m.	h. m.
	DERBY	8 0	11 30	2 15	4 15	9 0	8 0	5 30	9 0
	Willington	8 12	11 41	..	4 27	..	8 12	5 42	..
	Burton	8 25	11 53	2 38	4 40	9 25	8 25	5 55	9 25
	Barton and Walton ..	8 44	12 10	..	4 59	..	8 44	6 14	..
	Tamworth	9 7	12 32	3 17	5 22	10 7	9 7	6 37	10 7
	Kingsbury	9 26	12 49	..	5 41	..	9 26	6 56	..
	Coleshill	9 37	12 59	..	5 52	..	9 37	7 7	..
	Hampton	9 55	1 15	4 0	6 10	10 55	9 55	7 25	10 55
	BIRMINGHAM	10 30	1 45	4 30	6 40	11 30	10 30	8 0	11 30
	LONDON	3 30	6 45	9 30	11 30	5 30			5 30

LONDON AND BIRMINGHAM TO DERBY.	Birmingham § Mixed, 6¾ a.m.	§ 1st class with 2d class carriages, 6 a.m.	§ 1st and 2d class carriages only, 8¾ a.m.	§ Mixed, 1 p.m.	§ 1st class with 2d class carriages, 8½ p.m.	Birmingham Mixed, 7 a.m.	Birmingham § Mixed, 5½ p.m.	§ 1st class with 2d class carriages, 8½ p.m.
LONDON	..	6 0	8 45	1 0	8 30	..	..	8 30
BIRMINGHAM	6 45	10 30	1 0	5 45	2 30	7 0	5 30	2 30
Hampton	7 5	10 50	1 20	6 5	2 50	7 20	5 50	2 50
Coleshill	7 27	..	1 45	6 30	..	7 40	6 10	..
Kingsbury	7 36	..	1 56	6 41	..	7 55	6 25	..
Tamworth	7 50	11 35	2 13	6 58	3 43	8 10	6 40	3 43
Barton and Walton ..	8 12	..	2 38	7 23	..	8 35	7 5	..
Burton	8 27	12 12	2 55	7 40	4 25	8 52	7 22	4 25
Willington	8 43	..	3 12	7 57	..	9 10	7 40	..
DERBY	9 0	12 45	3 30	8 15	5 0	9 30	8 0	5 0

The trains marked thus § are in connexion with the trains of the Midland counties company between Derby and Nottingham; which (except on Sundays,) are further connected with coaches to and from all parts of the east.

Passengers are requested to be at the station ten minutes before the times advertised for starting. Carriages and horses must be at the station at least a quarter of an hour before.

LONDON & CROYDON RAILWAY.

From both places—8 5, 9, 10, and 12, in the morning. 2 20, 3 20, 4 20, 5 20, 6 20, 7 20, and 8 20 in the afternoon.

SUNDAY TRAINS

9 and 10 in the morning; and 2, 3, 4, 5, 6, 7, 8, and 9 in the afternoon.

1840 timetable.

Davis, surgeon of Coleshill was on the spot and attended to sufferers. Also Mr Hodgson of this town attended at the request of the company. The Earl of Aylesford at the conclusion of the inquest also committed the sub-contractor's foreman for neglect of duty. He was bailed."

Various company employees received acknowledgement from the directors for their prompt action at the site of the collision. Birkinshaw was commended. Allport and Kirtley received special thanks, as did Turner and Mills for restoring the line. On 14 July 1842 – coincidentally the day of Birkinshaw's farewell – a horse employed by John Stephens in waggoning on the line was struck by an engine and killed. On 2 January 1843 Thomas Docker threw an iron ball at a train at Coleshill in a foolish, rather than malicious manner. He was subsequently convicted under Lord Seymour's act, and sentenced to 6 months hard labour. On 6 March 1844 Samuel Higton fell from an engine and suffered a severely lacerated foot.

These events did not escape the notice of the railway press, and much was made of them by concerned individuals. Responsibility for the accidents were more often than not laid at the door of the directors, and a great deal of antagonism arose when matters of safety were compromised by the need for stringent management of finances. We shall hear now of one particularly fierce critic of the day.

Veritas Vincit

In December 1842 an inveterate letter writer appeared on the scene. A self-styled railway ombudsman, his outlets were *The Railway Times* and *The Railway Record*, and all letters were addressed from Birmingham. His pseudonym translates to "Truth will conquer", and his motto was from Shakespeare – "I do confess it is my nature's plague, To spy into abuses." He was careful to protect his anonymity, and became the cause of much anguish amongst the early railway administrators. His preferred target was railway superintendents and their like. He championed the causes of drivers and firemen, especially in relation to working conditions and wages. He thought so highly of himself that he had all his letters privately published in book form in 1847 under the title *Railway Locomotive Management*. Despite their anonymity, his letters have a sound ring of truth about them. The writer displays an amazingly detailed knowledge of operations within a number of railway companies, and for this reason the letters should be given credence.

It is the opinion of the present author that the source of these letters was John Robertson, of Birmingham. Who was John Robertson? The proprietor and editor of *The Railway Times* and subsequently *The Railway Record* no less! What better way to ensure publication of his letters? There are a number of clues which suggest Robertson – a rather pointed preface to the collected works – and the fact that when that gentleman took over the latter journal the letter-writer also switched his allegiance. The letters make fascinating, and illuminating reading. Written in an educated, lucid, and sometimes amusing style they struck home with unerring accuracy and embarrassing repetition. Viewed from a distance, perhaps some of the criticism was unfair, but the writer certainly got results.

Extracts from a few of the letters are provided here as an indication of his prodigious energy. Matthew Kirtley was a regular target, and even the worthy James Allport could not escape his hawk-like attention. During the summer of 1843 our correspondent accused Kirtley of various wrongdoings – imposing wage reductions on staff whilst augmenting his own salary; forcing unacceptably long working hours on drivers and firemen; instructing an employee to write contradictory letters (a correspondent possibly known as "M"); and using the company's errand boy for his personal business. Finally, he questioned his upbringing and right to hold the post of locomotive superintendent. Matthew Kirtley could no longer ignore the imputations. In August he wrote:

"Sir, – In yours of the 15th. inst., "Veritus Vincit" writing on locomotive management, states that Mr. Kirtley of the Birmingham and Derby Railway was bred a tailor. I beg to state distinctly that such was not the case; such a business for me was never contemplated. I am not ashamed of my origin, and have no wish to conceal it. I was born in Tanfield, county of Durham, where "V.V." can have full particulars. I am, Sir, yours &c., M Kirtley, Locomotive Superintendent Birmingham and Derby Junction Railway." The mis-spelling of *Veritas* caused some amusement. The next letter from "V.V." was a masterpiece.

Birmingham August 14 1843.
"Sir – In my last letter I mentioned that Mr. Matthew Kirtley, Superintendent of the Birmingham and Derby Railway, had employed one of his clerks to write to you a letter in contradiction of something I had advanced, and my information on this point, as on most others connected with Railway Management, turned out to be correct. When I read Mr. Kirtley's letter I certainly was not a little surprised, for it disclosed nothing, save that I had hurt his pride. He must not, however, blame me for the exposure; it was

your correspondent "M" that called it forth. Although surprised, I, at the same time, had much cause to feel flattered, for his letter went to corroborate the fact, that except as to the tailoring business, all I had stated was the *truth*, particularly that most glaring circumstance of the additional £100 per annum to his salary. The effect of the changes, at first, benefitting the proprietors to the amount of 2 3/4d. per annum for every £100 share, but now, not even *that*, for after a week's trial of the alteration, Mr. Kirtley was obliged to recall some of his discharged men, so that the proprietors are considerable losers; and, in addition to this loss, he has a draftsman engaged at 25s. per week. What he has to do with a draftsman I know not; if a draftsman be necessary, a superintendent could be found at a much less salary, and who would be possessed of other qualifications, *not* possessed by Mr. Kirtley.

As to the allegations that Mr. Kirtley had been originally a tailor, my informant may or may not be correct. I have seen him again, and he tells me that it was Mr. Kirtley himself that informed him when they were fellow-labourers at the Vulcan Foundry, that he tried the tailor trade, but found it would not *suit* him. No doubt he committed an error in saying that he had been *bred* a tailor, for the word "bred" would infer that he had served seven years' apprenticeship; and for that matter he was never *bred* to anything, certainly not to be a fit superintendent of the Birmingham and Derby Railway! He recommends me to go to the county of Durham for the particulars of his infant history. With that I and the public have nothing to do; but as to his history from his commencement on railways, I am of opinion I can give *that* much better than any one in the county of Durham, and I will try; but first of all, I wish it to be clearly understood that I have, and can have, no personal feeling against Mr. Matthew Kirtley, whose pretensions I am desirous of analyzing, simply because he is a fair specimen of a class now getting somewhat numerous.

The circumstances connected with his dismissal from the Leeds and Selby Railway afford another proof how the difference of situations alters men's minds. At the same time there was a very steady engine-driver of the name of Robson, and being possessed of considerable abilities, he was raised to be a foreman in the shed. This gave offence to Mr. Matthew Kirtley, who said (his own words) "I shall never submit to be lorded over by one of my equals;" and the consequence was, that a "strike" was agreed upon, if Robson were to be continued their superior. The names of those that "struck" were Kirtley, Kirkup, and

Hesketh; the other engineman, Isdale, would not join them. Mr. Kirtley and his then fireman went to all the other firemen, and begged them not to take an engine, for they were determined to stand out until Robson should be "reduced" again. After this the three *strikers* deputed Isdale to wait upon Mr. Smith, Civil Engineer of the line, to say (I will give you the exact words of what passed) that Kirtley, Kirkup, and Hesketh, would strike if Robson were continued foreman. Mr Smith answered, "Go and tell Kirtley, Kirkup, and Hesketh to go to * * * * if they choose." Mr Smith immediately went and ordered their instant dismissal! Would Mr. Matthew Kirtley have the goodness to answer the three following questions:-

1st. What would he say of his present engine-drivers were they to send a notice to the Directors, that unless Mr. Kirtley were reduced again to the rank of engine-driver they would strike?

2nd. When it was found necessary to remove the turn-tables that impeded the waggon-way to the goods-lift, why did he bury so many thousands of bricks, and refuse to take an offer that was made to him of from 15s. to 20s. per 1000, the purchaser to take them up and re-level at his own expense the ground, to Mr. Kirtley's entire satisfaction?

3rd. How many hours each day since he came to Birmingham does he owe the Company for the use of a lad from the shed to assist Mrs. Kirtley's servant in her kitchen, and run her messages?

In consequence of Mr Allport having identified himself with the management of Mr. Kirtley, I cannot but bring him also under review. In the first place, I must refer to the remark "that if he were appointed goods' manager, he would double the traffic over that of Mr. Dixon." The presumption of Mr. A. is unbounded, but he is not fit to "hold a candle" to Mr. Dixon, who, for integrity, intelligence, and general good management, cannot be surpassed, and is seldom equalled. I will give you a specimen of Mr. Allport's system of proceeding:- About two years an a half ago, a fatal accident took place on the Derby line, by a passenger train coming in contact with a plate-layer's "lurry," proceeding in an opposite direction on the same line. By the collision the train was thrown off the line, and a third class carriage overturned, in which were two of the Company's servants; one was killed on the spot, the other was severely injured. He had a wife and family, and was confined for a great length of time. When he was able to get out, Mr. Birkinshaw very humanely procured him a job which he was able to accomplish, namely to weigh the goods. When the late reductions took place, Mr. Allport and Mr. Kirtley removed this man up the line to attend some gates seven days in the week at 14s. a week. The man complained to these gentlemen that his wages were too low, and craved an advance; Mr. Allport replied that 10s. was too much for him, and told him to remain contented! Again, at Kingsbury station there was a clerk at 24s. per week, and a man to pump water for the engines at 21s. per week. At the reduction the waterman was discharged, and the duty of pumping the water was put upon the clerk, and at the same time his wages were reduced to 21s. per week. At the station that leads to Fazeley, the clerk there had 24s. per week. He was informed that his wages were to be reduced to 21s. He said that he could not do his duty efficiently at that rate, and resigned. The duty has since been performed by a porter. The clerk at Kingsbury complained of his heavy work, and perhaps because he was once coachman to D. Ledsam, Esq., he was removed to the Fazeley station, and the Kingsbury became vacant. A respectable individual applied for it; Mr Allport inquired what he would do the duty for? He said 30s. Mr. Allport told him he would not give more than 10s. per week, and *that* was quite enough for a man who was out of employment! No doubt these officials pique themselves on the "savings" they have effected, but for my own part I do not much admire the conduct of parties – "gentlemen" though they be – who can screw down their inferior's wages below the starving point, and at the same time apply for an increase of their own.

I have just learned that Mr. Allport's "saving" at the Kingsbury station, is, in practice, little to the interest of the Company. One day last week a train arrived at that station, when the fireman, not having the least idea that there was no water in the cistern, turned the cock of the pipe so much that he broke it. The following train arrived and wanted water; of course they could not obtain it, whereupon the driver pulled his fire out, not being aware that he had sufficient steam to carry him to the station (only thirteen miles). He had no alternative but to try his power, and fortunately, without fire, he reached the station in time. This, Sir, is the first-rate management of the Birmingham and Derby Company.

At Whitacre station, which is the point where the line leads to Hampton and Birmingham, and at which place, until last week, there was a watchman day and night to attend the points, part of the train has, during the day, to go off to Hampton, but during the night it is not so. Mr. Allport has paid off the night-watchman, directing the day-watchman to pin up the points. This may be very correct, so far as regards economy, but should any evil-disposed person connected with the village go to these points, take out the pins, and put them "half on," the whole train would be thrown off the line, with what probable results I need not say; or if the points were shifted "full on" in a dark or foggy night, the train would run on to Hampton instead of to Birmingham.

With respect to the turn-tables referred to in my letter, those namely which it was found necessary to remove and replace by larger tables in another place, under the direction of Mr. Kirtley, they are so situated that they must be removed again. A year's salary of Mr. Kirtley and Mr. Allport will not pay for this.

Such a system of management certainly confers little honour on the Board of Directors. If Mr. Allport does not amend his mode of managing the goods' traffic, I shall, at the request of a most respectable shareholder (although it will make me deviate from my usual course), address a letter to you upon his general management since he came to Birmingham.

I beg you to understand that I have no vindictive or malignant feeling against any superintendent whatever. As individuals I know them not; it is only in the performance of their public duty that I interfere with them, and when they adopt measures that have a tendency to put the travelling public in jeopardy of their lives, while such a system is continued, I shall not fail, with your friendly aid, to expose and denounce them."

And when it came to *royalty* – "V.V." was especially vigilant.

The visit of Queen Victoria

28 November 1843 was a highlight of operations on the Stonebridge Railway. On that day the young Queen Victoria and her consort Prince Albert travelled upon the line during their journey from Windsor to Drayton Manor, the home of Sir Robert Peel. Her Majesty was *en route* to Chatsworth, and it was her very first experience of rail travel upon the narrow gauge lines. Travelling arrangements were made by James Allport. Her train from Watford reached Hampton at 2.20 p.m. hauled by Bury locomotive No. 20 of the London and Birmingham railway. Upon arrival she was met by officials of the Birmingham and Derby company and presented with a red velvet

THE QUEEN IN 1843.

Mary Evans Picture Library

Queen Adelaide's carriage at the NRM.

scrolled map as a memento of her visit. The train itself comprised three plain flat trucks, upon which carriages were conveyed; four coaches; and the Queen's saloon carriage, which had mounted upon its roof a very large and ornate crown. Whilst the presentations were being made, a Birmingham and Derby locomotive replaced the Bury engine. Five minutes later, at 2.25 p.m. the royal train departed towards Coleshill hauled by the Mather Dixon engine *Burton*, driven by Matthew Kirtley himself. No time was lost, for Tamworth was reached at a quarter to three, but for twenty brief minutes the branch line basked in royal glory. The following train also conveyed royalty, the dowager Queen Adelaide, accompanied by the Duke of Wellington. Queen Victoria's Journal contains the following entry for the day.

"We passed Crick, Wilton, Rugby (where all the schoolboys were out), Brandon, Coventry, & Hampton. At the latter place we stopped, in order to go upon another line. Everything was extremely well managed on the railroad, & the train goes along very easily, though not quite so fast as the Gt. Western."

Clearly her earlier trip along Brunel's billiard table broad gauge line to the West had impressed her sense of speed. Her visit to the Midlands was covered in great depth by *The Illustrated London News* and that journal also provides and excellent description of the royal saloon. Sadly, this carriage was not preserved, but at least No. 2, Queen Adelaide's carriage, can be seen in the National Railway Museum, York. The whole visit was a great success. Smooth though events were on the day, our venomous friend "V.V." could not let matters pass without comment. He wrote:

Birmingham, December 12 1843
"At first sight, I have no doubt you will say, what has the Queen's visit to do with locomotive management? But it gives a beautiful illustration of some of my former allegations against certain parties, as to their unfitness for the important offices they hold. When it was announced that her Majesty was to be at Watford on a certain day, Mr. Bury, Locomotive Superintendent of the London and

Birmingham Railway, did not find it necessary to order any particular engine to be put in the shed, to undergo a special repair to convey Royalty down the line. That gentleman manages to have his engines kept in such a thorough state of repair that I believe it would matter little as to safety what engine might be fixed upon. There is, no doubt, a difference in some of them with regard to power, but not as to being in an efficient state. When the news reached the Birmingham and Derby, Mr. Matthew Kirtley was "put upon his pins." He ordered the *Burton* engine to be taken into the shed, and completely overhauled, in case she might break down, for he had not confidence in any of his stock to convey Royalty. When his brother, Mr. Thomas Kirtley, of the North Midland, heard the news, he was also obliged to resort to the same expedient as his brother Mr. Matthew. He ordered No. 20 into the shed, and that engine underwent repair. But when the tidings reached the ears of Mr. Josiah Kearsley, Locomotive Superintendent on the Midland Counties, he was, like Mr. Bury, quite prepared; for he keeps the whole of his engines in such perfect order, that he is ready to convey

Royalty at a moment's notice any day.

If there be an honour in conducting an engine when Royalty is in the train, then certainly Mr. Kearsley can claim that honour above all other Superintendents in the kingdom. He was not like Mr. M. Kirtley, who had with him on the foot-plate an experienced engineman and one or two others, and yet gave it out to the Editors of the papers that he conducted the engine, when it was no such thing. Mr. Thomas Kirtley of the North Midland did the same. Mr. Kearsley on the two occasions, drove her Majesty and suite. He took a fireman on the foot-plate with him, put on a jacket, and conducted the engine himself; thereby showing, as I formerly stated, that he is truly a practical as well as a theoretical Superintendent."

Certainly "V.V." represented fairly the fears of many, and by this time the pages of the papers and journals were littered with letters from worried shareholders regarding the parlous state of the company's finances. So now we turn from glory to the grim realities of survival.

INTERIOR OF THE ROYAL RAILWAY CARRIAGE.

Mary Evans Picture Library

CHAPTER SIX

The Years of Conflict

Revenue

For the convenience of running their trains along the London and Birmingham's line from Hampton to Birmingham the company had to pay a toll of 1s.6d. per person carried. The fare for local passengers on that section was 3s.0d., so half was taken up by the toll. The receipts for the first fortnight were £1328 10s.8d., including tolls of £162 14s.0d. The amount of toll paid for goods on the Hampton to Birmingham line is uncertain, but the author suggests that 1 3/8d. per ton per mile would have been appropriate, as this was the rate charged by the Grand Junction Railway. Whatever it was, it can be assumed to have been substantial, and a further significant drain on resources. Between Hampton and London a toll of 4s. per ton was levied on ale from Burton. The effect of these tolls on the company's finances over the next three years became almost too great for them to bear. A subsequent attempt to get them reduced was met with uncompromising indifference by the London and Birmingham company. There was to be no respite from this burden until February 1842 when their own direct line into Birmingham was completed. This line branched off at Whitacre and followed the Tame valley before terminating at Lawley Street, where a large station was built.

The average weekly gross receipts for the company up to 1841 were about £750, of which £160 was paid in tolls. Allport's returns for Hampton on 14/15 November 1840 show takings of £9 0s. 7d. and £2 4s. 7d. After payment of tolls very little was left to cover working expenses, let alone pay shareholders a good dividend. Matters improved slightly towards 1843, and in July of that year there are three consecutive weeks of £888, £2619, and £952. The middle one, week ending 15 July, was the occasion of the Derby Agricultural Show and brought much extra traffic. Additional trains from London stopped at Hampton, and the London and Birmingham reduced their cattle rates by a third. (But not those for two-legged passengers – the L&B were too hard-nosed for that.)

The average fare in old pence per mile for passengers during the second half of 1843 was 2.76, 2.09, and 1.55 for the three classes of travel. Horses cost 4.10, carriages 7.41, cattle 6.30 and all goods 2.21.

Some idea of the paucity of the company's finances can be gained from a comparison of working expenses. On the Birmingham and Derby Junction Railway they accounted for 74.2% of all income. On the London and Birmingham the equivalent figure was 37.4%. And this was the state of affairs *before* any competition started.

The returns of 31 December 1842 show 219 employees on the company's books with an annual wage bill of £14,716. For an undertaking of 48 1/2 route miles this was seen as an unaffordable luxury, and wide-ranging economies were implemented. We have seen how critics reacted to the wage reductions. The need for these reductions was largely brought about by loss of revenue when other, competing railways opened for traffic. What resulted was the first rate war in railway history.

The tariff war

By June 1840 the company had established itself firmly on the railway map. For ten months it had enjoyed a monopoly on traffic passing between London and the North. On 1 July of that year the North Midland railway opened its lines from Derby to Leeds and beyond. This immediately gave the Birmingham and Derby company access to yet more passengers and goods. There was just one problem. On that day the Midland Counties' line from Rugby to Derby was also opened. This route was some 11 miles shorter than the one *via* Coventry and Hampton. Clearly the public would choose the shorter route in the absence of any financial incentive to stay with the Birmingham company. The Directors had, of course, anticipated this event, and on 25 June attempted to come to an agreement with their counterparts at the Midland Counties on the subjects of fares and the division of traffic, but to no avail.

A battle for traffic now seemed inevitable. The Birmingham and Derby company's early confidence in winning such a war was based upon the following reasoning, and this is how they reassured shareholders. As their line, and that of the London and Birmingham company were to have been constructed *entirely for other purposes*, and with a remunerating profit attached to each, then any additional traffic (not accounted for in parliamentary estimates) must generate revenue over and above that necessary to defray working expenses and interest charges. By contrast, the Midland Counties Railway between Rugby and Derby was to be constructed mainly for the purpose of carrying passengers and goods between those two towns. Their works were heavier, and gradients marginally worse. The Hampton branch was executed very cheaply, of that there is no doubt. Despite the 11 mile disadvantage, therefore, the Birmingham and Derby company felt able to challenge the Midland Counties without jeopardising their own financial standing.

The Midland Counties and the North Midland had, however, the 1838 agreement to share trade upon the opening of the Rugby to Derby line, and the Midland Counties considered this agreement to be their guarantee of winning any conflict. The Birmingham and Derby directors challenged its exclusive interpretation, and the North Midland had to sullenly concede that the agreement only held force whilst no other company offered *cheaper, speedier* routes. With the anticipation of income from the traffic on the north-east to south-west routes, the directors of the Birmingham company felt confident of meeting the long-term expectations of their shareholders. But the Gloucester route was not yet open. As they had already captured the London traffic, they had at all costs to retain the patronage of it. And so now they were prepared to undercut their opponents to whatever degree proved necessary, even to bring about their ruin.

The Midland Counties' directors, for their part, immediately advised their own shareholders of the inaccuracy of this reasoning, pointing out that their railway had in fact a much wider base from which to draw traffic. They still saw the agreement with the North Midland as binding, even though that company had to admit that it was dependent upon factors such as competitive rates and speeds. From that date the North Midland paid scant regard to the arrangements for working connecting trains at Derby for the Birmingham and Derby's traffic, and offered only grudging co-operation on fares and rates to the Birmingham company. Relations between all three now deteriorated rapidly.

James Allport devised a scale of differential fares to overcome the disadvantage of distance.

The normal fares between Derby and Hampton were 8s. first-class and 6s. second-class. He reduced these fares (for both classes of travel) to 1s. 6d., but *for through passengers only*. The fares between London and Derby were thus set at 29s. first-class and 19s. 6d. second-class. The London and Birmingham charged 5s. for carrying passengers between Rugby and Hampton. This meant that the Midland Counties could charge a maximum of 6s. 6d. for the equivalent journey *via* Leicester if they were to successfully compete. They could, though, reduce their charge to 5s. which would effectively force the Birmingham company to carry their passengers *free of charge*. They were apparently not of a mind to relinquish vitally needed revenue that willingly though, and as Allport's stratagem was considered illegal by the Midland Counties' directors, they persuaded the Attorney General to challenge it in the Court of Chancery.

On 8 August 1840 the application was heard by the Lord Chancellor and dismissed with costs. He decided that the proceedings were in accordance with the Birmingham and Derby Junction's Act, and that it would be improper "to prevent the public from enjoying the advantages of cheap travelling, under the pretence that such interference was for the benefit of the public". After that the Midland Counties had no option but to fight.

Comic situations arose. Passengers from Derby to Coventry *via* Rugby could travel for 5s. on the Midland Counties line, but that company insisted upon charging a fare of 7s. for the Derby to Leicester section. Not surprisingly, travellers to Leicester bought tickets for Coventry and then attempted to alight at their preferred destination, only to be prevented from so doing by the company's officers!

The long term effects of the prolonged struggle were ruinous to both concerns. Either was prepared to suffer a loss provided that of its rival was greater. In 1843 the Midland Counties tried again to halt the madness, and succeeded in obtaining a writ of *Mandamus* from the Queen's Bench division, which compelled the Birmingham and Derby company to equalise fares and abandon the differential arrangement.

The final irony of this crippling conflict is the failure of the Midland Counties to build the Clay Cross extension that they had gone to so much trouble to justify. Pressure was being exerted from the North Midland and others, and the Midland Counties' Act of Incorporation was considered to have insufficient authority to actually proceed with the venture. Eventually though, common sense won the day, and all parties were forced to come to terms. We now enter a phase in the chronicling of the

Extract from staff returns - Birmingham and Derby Junction Railway
31 December 1842

GENERAL MANAGEMENT

General Manager - John Dixon   £500 p.a.

SECRETARY AND AUDIT

Secretary and Cashier - Thomas Kell   £400 p.a.
Audit Superintendent   £150 p.a.
Office Boy   £15 13s 0d p.a.

LOCOMOTIVE

Locomotive Superintendent - Matthew Kirtley   £200 p.a.
Engine-drivers   Grade 1   7s 0d per duty
                   Grade 5   4s 0d per duty

COACHING

Station Master   £100 p.a.
Guards   £1 6s 0d p.w.
Errand Boy   5s 0d p.w.

GOODS

Goods Superintendent - James Allport   £150 p.a.
Messenger   8s 0d p.w.

CARRIAGE REPAIR

Carriage Superintendent   £2 0s 0d p.w.

Between	12 Aug. 1839			8 July 1840			13 Feb. 1843			3 Apr. 1843		
	1st	2nd	3rd	1st	2nd	3rd	1st	2nd	3rd	1st	2nd	3rd
London and Derby .	35s.	24s.	..	29s.	19s. 6d.	..	30s.	20s.	14s.	28s.	19s.	14s.
Birmingham and Derby . .	10s.	7s.	5s.	10s.	7s.	5s.	11s.	8s.	6s.	11s.	8s.	6s.
Hampton and Derby	8s.	6s.	4s. 6d.	8s.	6s.	4s. 6d.	8s.	6s.	4s. 6d.	8s.	6s.	4s. 6d.

Fares during the tariff war.

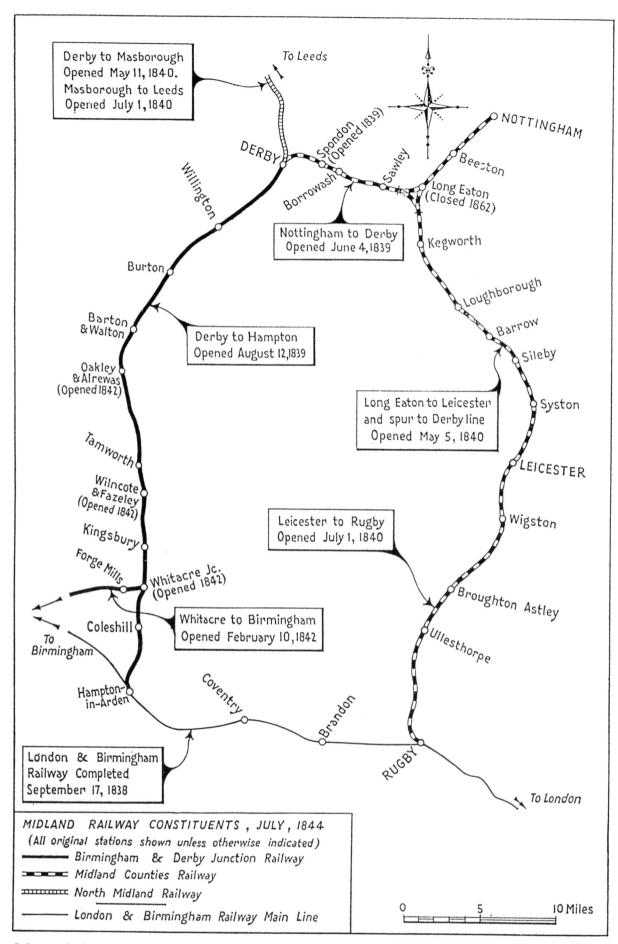

Map of the constituents of the Midland Railway in July, 1844, showing the connections with the London & Birmingham Railway at Hampton-in-Arden and Rugby

Within the map:

Derby to Masborough Opened May 11, 1840. Masborough to Leeds Opened July 1, 1840

To Leeds

Spondon (Opened 1839)

NOTTINGHAM

Beeston

Long Eaton (Closed 1862)

Nottingham to Derby Opened June 4, 1839

Sawley

Borrowash

DERBY

Willington

Kegworth

Burton

Loughborough

Barton & Walton

Barrow

Derby to Hampton Opened August 12, 1839

Sileby

Oakley & Alrewas (Opened 1842)

Long Eaton to Leicester and spur to Derby line Opened May 5, 1840

Syston

Tamworth

LEICESTER

Wilncote & Fazeley (Opened 1842)

Wigston

Kingsbury

Leicester to Rugby Opened July 1, 1840

Forge Mills

Whitacre Jc. (Opened 1842)

Broughton Astley

Coleshill

Whitacre to Birmingham Opened February 10, 1842

Ullesthorpe

To Birmingham

Hampton-in-Arden

Coventry

Brandon

RUGBY

London & Birmingham Railway Completed September 17, 1838

To London

MIDLAND RAILWAY CONSTITUENTS, JULY, 1844
(All original stations shown unless otherwise indicated)
— Birmingham & Derby Junction Railway
— Midland Counties Railway
— North Midland Railway
— London & Birmingham Railway Main Line

0   5   10 Miles

E

Stonebridge Railway that has little parallel in railway history.

Into Birmingham

On 10 February 1842 the line from Whitacre to Birmingham was opened for traffic into the new station at Lawley Street. Although an inclined spur to the Grand Junction Railway was opened in the following April to allow access to that line, a problem existed with the nearby terminus of the Birmingham and Gloucester Railway. The Lawley Street station had been built at a level 40 feet lower than the adjacent lines, thus making transfer of goods between the Birmingham and Gloucester railway extremely cumbersome. To overcome these difficulties various goods lifts were installed from July 1843 onwards to raise and lower wagons between the two levels. They were inefficient and matters were never completely satisfactory until physical connection was achieved in the 1850s.

At the junction of the Hampton branch and the direct line a small station was built at Whitacre. It was situated opposite the *Railway Inn*, but unfortunately nothing remains of it today. The effect of the opening of the direct line to Birmingham was twofold. Firstly, the company enjoyed immediate relief from the toll payments paid to the London and Birmingham. Secondly, the importance of the Hampton branch was significantly reduced. So much so that the double track line between Hampton and Whitacre was singled. Between August 1842 and March 1843 a line of track was lifted, and The Stonebridge Railway became the first main line in Britain to achieve this distinction.

The case for amalgamation

Despite success in opening the new line, the fortunes of the Birmingham and Derby Junction Railway were in a poor state. Economies were made by reducing wages and staffing levels, but the company could never have been regarded as profitable. During the period 1840 – 1844 their dividends were very low – averaging 1.6%. The Midland Counties were little better at 2.75%, and the North Midland 3.5%. Success was measured against the performance of the London and Birmingham, who averaged a comparable dividend of a healthy 10%. Clearly the shareholders of the warring companies were dissatisfied with the disastrously unhealthy competition that was being carried on. Not unnaturally, many of them had interests in all three concerns, and were horrified at the profligate activities of their companies' officers. Suggestions were put forward that The North Midland, and then the London and Birmingham, should take over the running of the two smaller railways.

Before these could reach concrete form however, George Hudson, chairman of the York and North Midland Railway, laid before all three sets of shareholders comprehensive and equitable proposals for amalgamation. "The Grand Juggler", "The Railway King", were epithets applied equally to this charismatic individual, but his eye for business was never in doubt. His plans were welcomed by all, and so on 10 May 1844 hostilities formally ceased with the formation of The Midland Railway.

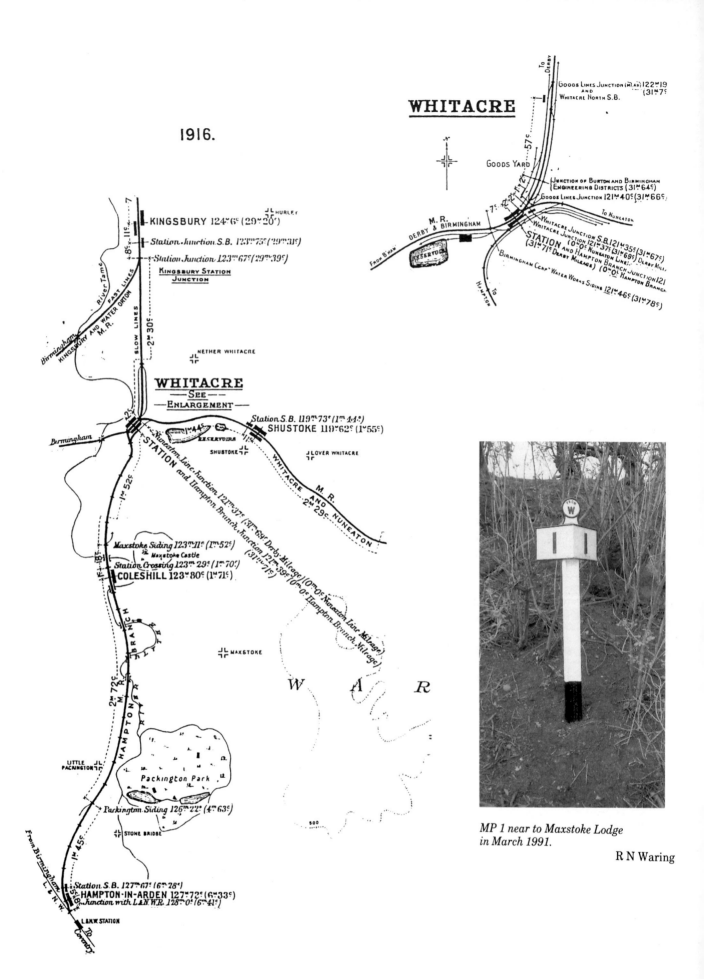

WHITACRE

1916.

KINGSBURY 124ᵐ6ᶜ (29ᵐ20ᶜ) ⌐HURLEY

Station Junction S.B. 123ᵐ73ᶜ (29ᵐ31ᶜ)

Station Junction 123ᵐ67ᶜ (29ᵐ39ᶜ)

KINGSBURY STATION JUNCTION

Goods Lines Junction (M.R.) 122ᵐ19
AND WHITACRE NORTH S.B. (31ᵐ79ᶜ)

GOODS YARD

JUNCTION OF BURTON AND BIRMINGHAM
(ENGINEERING DISTRICTS (31ᵐ64ᶜ)
GOODS LINES JUNCTION 121ᵐ40ᶜ (31ᵐ66ᶜ)

To Nuneaton

WHITACRE JUNCTION S.B.121ᵐ35ᶜ (31ᵐ67ᶜ)
WHITACRE JUNCTION 121ᵐ37ᶜ (31ᵐ69ᶜ) DERBY MIL.
STATION (0·0ᶜ NUNEATON LINE) (31ᵐ69ᶜ)
(31ᵐ71ᶜ DERBY MILEAGE)
AND HAMPTON BRANCH JUNCTION 121
(0·0ᶜ HAMPTON BRANCH)
BIRMINGHAM CORP⁵ WATER WORKS SIDING 121ᵐ46ᶜ (31ᵐ78ᶜ)

WHITACRE
— SEE —
ENLARGEMENT

NETHER WHITACRE

Station S.B. 119ᵐ73ᶜ (1ᵐ44ᶜ)
SHUSTOKE 119ᵐ62ᶜ (1ᵐ55ᶜ)

LOVER WHITACRE

Nuneaton Line Junction 121ᵐ37ᶜ (31ᵐ64ᶜ Derby Mileage) (0ᵐ·0ᶜ Nuneaton Line Mileage)
STATION and Hampton Branch Junction 121ᵐ39ᶜ (0ᵐ·0ᶜ Hampton Branch Mileage) (31ᵐ71ᶜ)

Maxstoke Siding 123ᵐ11ᶜ (1ᵐ52ᶜ)
Maxstoke Castle
Station Crossing 123ᵐ29ᶜ (1ᵐ70ᶜ)
COLESHILL 123ᵐ80ᶜ (1ᵐ71ᶜ)

MAXSTOKE

W   A   R

Packington Siding 126ᵐ22ᶜ (4ᵐ63ᶜ)

LITTLE PACKINGTON

Packington Park

STONE BRIDGE

500

Station S.B. 127ᵐ67ᶜ (6ᵐ28ᶜ)
HAMPTON-IN-ARDEN 127ᵐ72ᶜ (6ᵐ33ᶜ)
Junction with L & N.W.R. 128ᵐ0ᶜ (6ᵐ41ᶜ)

L. & N.W. STATION

MP 1 near to Maxstoke Lodge
in March 1991.

R N Waring

Taken from the Midland Railway Distance Diagrams, 1916.

CHAPTER SEVEN

Operational Running from 1844

Midland style

The Midland Railway had a policy of expansion. This was particularly so in respect of goods traffic. It was prepared to lay sidings wherever they were likely to be worthwhile. Passengers mattered too. It furnished stations with all the niceties expected of them, and Midland Railway coaches came to represent the last word in travelling comfort. It set high standards. Even in the smallest matter, for example mileposts. An act of 1845 required all companies to erect distance posts at every quarter-mile for the purposes of calculating rates, and this branch had Midland style cast iron posts of a very pleasing appearance. Fortunately a number have survived, and have been restored.

Allport's influence was wide-ranging. Covered seats for all classes of passenger. Third-class coaches on all trains at a penny a mile. Abolition of second-class. Other railway companies squealed in anguish at these measures, but Allport was resolute, and his policies paid off. The Midland captured the hearts of the travelling public, and profits boomed. He also rationalised the movement of goods in the larger yards where dissent and frustration were rife.

Midland influence upon the Stonebridge Railway was not great, as the line's prestige was short-lived, but there are still traces of that bygone age to be found.

Development of the line

The Midland Railway continued to provide services to Derby on the line, but at a much reduced frequency. On 1 November 1864 the line from Nuneaton to Birmingham was opened. It met the Birmingham and Derby line at Whitacre 3/4 mile south of the 1842 junction. As a result the deviation spur was removed, although the original station was probably not demolished until 1877. A new, larger station was provided, and the junction took on increasing importance. The incoming line from Hampton was re-laid so as to approach on a curve into the southern end of the platforms. The lines from Derby and Nuneaton converged at the northern end of the station, where lengthy goods lay-by sidings were provided. To the south of the station a cattle and carriage loading dock was built. Interchange sidings for the Hampton line were laid, plus goods sidings for the Derby and Nuneaton lines. The adjacent pumping station of Birmingham Water Corporation was also provided with its own access. The main station building on the island platform was of single storey brick built construction, with a small timber framed waiting room being provided on the single platform opposite. A wrought iron lattice footbridge connected the platforms, and barrow crossings were laid at the foot of the ramps. Two water tanks were installed – one at the meeting of the Derby and Nuneaton lines, and another at the start of the Hampton branch. Near to the site of the original Birmingham and Derby station a weighbridge and a coal siding were installed.

The rather extended layout that resulted eventually demanded two signal boxes; one controlling the station and junctions, built at the north end of the platforms some time before 1877; and another to the north of the site on the Derby line close to the site of the 1842 station. The latter opened on 7 November 1897, and controlled the goods lay-by lines.

Whitacre Junction box was replaced on 30 April 1899, and Whitacre North box was re-framed on 27 May 1900. In 1909 a cut-off line was built from Kingsbury to Water Orton *via* Lea Marston, thus bypassing Whitacre junction, and further reducing the importance of the branch. Goods traffic was diverted on 22 March, with passenger services following suit on 3 May.

In 1873 the block telegraph system was introduced between Whitacre and Coleshill, but not, however, between Coleshill and Hampton. No communication of any sort ever existed to connect these stations, neither block bells nor telephone. At Coleshill, signal levers were installed adjacent to the now disused "down" platform, and despite appearing in the record books in a list of "signal posts" it is possible that there was never a signal box structure. Although two home and two distant signals were erected, it was common practice to pass

'Midland Style'. A barrow boy at Derby displays the company's wares.

National Railway Museum

A Whitacre – Hampton train awaits departure in 1902. Johnson 0-6-0 Nº 2641 heads the solitary Clayton 40ft brake composite. A Derby or Nuneaton train with clerestory coach is alongside.

Lens of Sutton

Coleshill station in 1916. The signal levers are well displayed, and the old up platform nicely kept. The station was still in use for passenger services.

Authors' collection

The daily passenger train poses at Coleshill in May 1916. Johnson 0-6-0 Nº 3678 hauls the single coach.

National Railway Museum

Coleshill station in 1921, after closure to passengers.

Courtesy R S Carpenter

Maxstoke station in 1936. Still tidily maintained despite its lack of traffic.

Authors' collection

the home signals at danger.

A single siding for the storage of up to ten wagons was installed here in 1883. Access was controlled by a separate ground frame. It was here that the long-established firm of Rollasons' coal merchants started trading, with an office, weighbridge, and a fleet of three private wagons. Started by Harriet Rollason, the grandmother of the present owner Phil Rollason, the firm celebrated their centenary in 1984, and played a major part in the history of the line.

With the expansion of trade towards the end of the nineteenth-century, goods sidings were also laid c. 1900 to serve the large estates of Maxstoke and Packington, again being worked by ground frames. The Maxstoke Castle siding was situated just to the north of Coleshill station, and a farm path crosses the bed of both the old running line and siding at this point. The estate siding held perhaps eight wagons, with coal coming in and timber going out.

The siding at Packington also took coal, and in addition received live (freshly killed) fish from Grimsby. The contents of the fish-wagons were transferred to four salt-water tanks located in the grounds of Packington Hall. The remains of the old stop-block at the end of this siding can still be observed.

Severe storms on the last day of 1900 caused widespread damage due to flooding. The timber river bridges were badly weakened, and a number had to be strengthened. B e t w e e n Maxstoke siding and Coleshill station was the large bridge over the River Blythe. A farm accommodation underbridge adjacent to it frequently flooded due to the low level of the surrounding farmland, and silted up to the distress of the cattle that used it. In 1922, after complaints, the Midland Railway raised the level of the roadway beneath this bridge.

At Hampton significant developments occurred, despite the singling of the line. It remained a busy junction, and passengers awaiting connections there must have enjoyed the hospitality provided, especially as alcoholic refreshments could be taken! Although the locomotive shed had declined in use after engineering operations had moved to Birmingham in about 1842, the site remained intact. The next recorded use of this building is in 1884 when it was let to Wyckham Blackwell, a local timber, coal and corn merchant. He was no slouch, for he is named as the licensee of *The Stonebridge Hotel* in 1892. His successors continue to trade successfully at Hampton to this day, having purchased the site from British Rail in 1971, and the development of their business is part of the folklore of the Stonebridge Railway. The buildings were used as a saw mill and workshops. Behind the main

shed were two short sidings and a goods yard. A weighbridge and office faced onto the adjacent lane. A dock siding was built for loading cattle. At the end of this siding was positioned a loading gauge. Four signals were erected; two at the south end of the station to permit access from and to the main line; a home signal at the north end of the station platform to give clearance on the branch; and a fixed distant signal at milepost 5 3/4. The successor to the London and Birmingham Railway company, the London and North Western Railway, operated Hampton station jointly with the Midland Railway, and train movements were controlled from a small signal box positioned to the north the station platform. Up to 1849 Hampton was also known as "Derby Junction". From 1 November 1849 it changed to Hampton Junction, and on 1 December 1872 it became plain Hampton.

On 28 July 1884 the joint arrangements ceased, and on 1 September following the LNWR opened a new station on the site of the present day one. From this date, passengers were obliged to use the new station, although the Midland station continued to handle goods. For a time both stations were called Hampton, but in July 1886, to avoid confusion, the LNWR changed theirs to Hampton-in-Arden. Around 1890 the LNWR built a new signal box on the "down" side of the London to Birmingham line. This box then took control of traffic on and off the branch.

Name changes were not uncommon elsewhere. On 1 November 1849 Coleshill became Coleshill (Hampton Line), but on 1 December 1872 it was back to plain Coleshill. 1 October 1904 saw Whitacre Junction renamed Whitacre, possibly in connection with an accident just prior to that date.

At the grouping on 1 January 1923, and the creation of "the Big Four", the London Midland and Scottish Railway succeeded as operators of the line. Coleshill station was renamed Maxstoke on 9 July 1923, its original name being transferred to Forge Mills on the Water Orton line. At about this time it seems that the line was re-surveyed, for before 1938 all the quarter-mile posts were moved, by increasing degrees, nearer to Whitacre. They marked the distances from Whitacre Junction, at which point milepost 0 still proudly stands. The Whitacre Junction signal box was renewed in 1939.

Locomotives and rolling stock

The early Kirtley 0-6-0 design of engines ran on the railway, as evidenced by the 1875 photograph of Hampton. Whether or not his 2-4-0 locomotive did is uncertain. The mainstay

COLESHILL

Based on an official 1883 plan for the installation of the new connection and siding at Coleshill station. The ground frame was bolt locked by Annett's key attached to the train staff.

Coleshill track plan

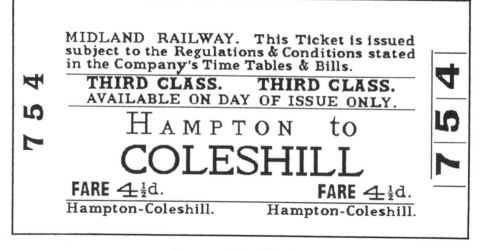

Coleshill Group

MIDLAND RAILWAY. This Ticket is issued
subject to the Regulations & Conditions stated
in the Company's Time Tables & Bills.

THIRD CLASS.   THIRD CLASS.
AVAILABLE ON DAY OF ISSUE ONLY.

HAMPTON   to
COLESHILL

FARE 4½d.   FARE 4½d.
Hampton-Coleshill.   Hampton-Coleshill.

754   754

Hampton – Coleshill ticket

[Passenger & Goods]   WHITACRE TO HAMPTON.

Distance (Mls.)	STATIONS.	1 Passenger A.M. ARR.	DEP.	2 Mineral A.M. ARR.	DEP.	3 Passenger P.M. ARR.	DEP.	4 Passenger P.M. ARR.	DEP.	5 Passenger P.M. ARR.	DEP.	6 Passenger P.M. ARR.	DEP.
..	WHITACRE	..	9 30	..	10 50	..	12 50	..	2 20	..	5 40	....	....
2	Coleshill	9 38	9 40	11 0	..	12 58	1 0	2 28	2 30	5 48	5 50	....	....
7½	HAMPTON	10 5	..	11 20	..	1 20	..	2 50	..	6 10	..	....	....

[Passenger & Goods]   HAMPTON TO WHITACRE.

Distance (Mls.)	STATIONS.	1 Mineral A.M. ARR.	DEP.	2 Passenger A.M. ARR.	DEP.	3 Passenger P.M. ARR.	DEP.	4 Passenger P.M. ARR.	DEP.	5 Passenger P.M. ARR.	DEP.	6 Passenger P.M. ARR.	DEP.
..	HAMPTON	..	8 30	..	10 20	..	..	..	3 20	..	7 15	....	....
5½	Coleshill	8 50	..	10 32	10 33	..	..	3 20	3 22	7 25	7 27	....	....
7½	WHITACRE	9 0	..	10 40	..	..	..	3 40	..	7 35	..	....	....

Printed by W. Bemrose and Son, Derby.   1853

WHITACRE TO HAMPTON.

Distance (Miles)	STATIONS.	1 Pass. a.m.	2 Mineral a.m.	3 Pass. p.m.	4 Pass. p.m.	5 Pass. p.m.
..	WHITACRE	9 30	10 50	12 5	..	6 5
2	Coleshill	9 40	..	12 13	..	6 10
7½	HAMPTON	10 5	11 20	12 30	..	6 25

HAMPTON TO WHITACRE.

Distance (Miles)	STATIONS.	1 Mineral a.m.	2 Pass. a.m.	3 Pass. p.m.	4 Pass. p.m.	5
..	HAMPTON	8 10	10 20	3 30	7 15	..
5½	Coleshill	8 ..	10 33	3 43	7 25	..
7½	WHITACRE	8 40	10 40	3 50	7 35	..

1856

WHITACRE TO HAMPTON.

Distance (Miles)	STATIONS.	1 Pass. & Goods. a.m.	2 Pass. & Goods. p.m.	3 Pass. p.m.	4 Pass. & Goods. p.m.	5 Pass. & Goods. p.m.
..	WHITACRE	8 45	12 5	3 5	6 50	8 30
2	Coleshill	8 55	12 10	3 1	6 56	8 36
7½	HAMPTON	9 10	12 26	3 25	7 10	8 50

The Hampton Engine must take Traffic from the New to the Old Whitacre Station at 10.30 a.m. & 2.50 p.m. No. 5 Train waits for Burton Goods when required.

HAMPTON TO WHITACRE.

Distance (Miles)	STATIONS.	6 Pass. & Goods. a.m.	7 Pass. & Goods. a.m.	8 Pass. p.m.	9 Pass. & Goods. p.m.	10 Pass. & Goods. p.m.
..	HAMPTON	7 30	9 25	2 25	3 55	7 55
5½	Coleshill	7 42	9 38	2 27	4 8	8 8
7½	WHITACRE	7 50	9 44	2 45	4 15	8 15

1877

WHITACRE TO HAMPTON.

Distance (Miles)	STATIONS.	87 Pass. & Goods. a.m.	88	89	90	91
..	WHITACRE	8 30	..	..	..	..
2	Coleshill	8 45	..	..	..	..
6½	HAMPTON	9 0	..	..	..	..

HAMPTON TO WHITACRE.

Distance (Miles)	STATIONS.	92	93 Pass. & Goods. a.m.	94	95	96
..	HAMPTON	..	10 15	..	..	..
5½	Coleshill	..	10 37	..	..	..
6½	WHITACRE	..	10 45	..	..	..

1877

HAMPTON AND WHITACRE.

WEEKDAYS.							WEEKDAYS.					
Leamington (L. & N. W.) — dep.	7 20	..	..	..	..	—	Derby — dep.	6 28	..	..	..	..
Coventry (L. & N. W.)	8 16						Burton	6 50				
HAMPTON — dep.	8 40	..	..	..	..	—	WHITACRE — dep.	8 10	..	..	..	..
Coleshill	8 50						Coleshill	8 17				
WHITACRE — arr.	8 55	..	..	..	..	—	HAMPTON — arr.	8 25	..	..	..	..
Burton — arr.	11 57						Coventry (L. & N. W.) — arr.	9 35				
Derby —	12 18						Leamington (L. & N. W.) —	10 25				

1916

MIDLAND RAILWAY.

ORDER No. 47.   Derby, April 26th, 1855.

Poultry, &c., not to be kept at Stations.

In consequence of the numerous complaints made to the Directors by persons forwarding grain and others, of the loss of and damage to grain by the Poultry, &c., allowed to range over the Stations and Warehouses, they have ordered that no Poultry, Pigeons, Pigs, or other animals of a similar description shall be allowed to be kept upon or have access to the Company's premises.

From this date to the 15th May, will be allowed for the disposal of any Stock now kept by the Company's Servants; after which date you are required to see this order attended to at your Station.

There may be some places where there would be no objection to Stock being kept, but in these cases application must be made to, and permission obtained from me, before it can be allowed.

Keep this Order, affix it in your Order-book, and acknowledge receipt of it on annexed Form.

JAMES ALLPORT, General-Manager.

Mr. _____

_____ Station.

MR Livestock Notice

Midland Railway.

GENERAL-MANAGER'S OFFICE,
Derby, December 22nd, 1868.

ORDER No. 233.

DEAR SIR,

Exhibition of Fare Tables for Information of Passengers.

An Act of Parliament passed during the last Session, provides that the Passenger Fares in operation at each Station shall be exhibited to the Public in every Booking Office.

Framed List of the Fares in operation from your Station will be sent you to-morrow, which must be fixed up immediately on receipt, in a position accessible to the Public, but out of the reach of Children, and persons likely to be mischievous or to damage them.

When fares are revised or new fares quoted, the lists must be carefully and neatly corrected. A spare column has been introduced in each case, and when the first correction is made, a pen must be drawn through the old figures, and the new ones inserted in the spare column. Subsequent corrections may be made by erasing the old figures and substituting the revised ones in the same place. When Fares are quoted to new Stations, the names of such new Stations must be inserted in alphabetical order.

If you notice any discrepancy between the Fares entered on the Table and those you are charging, correct the former, and call my attention to the matter.

Keep this Order, affix it in your order book and acknowledge receipt of it on annexed Form.

JAMES ALLPORT,
GENERAL-MANAGER.

Mr. _____

_____ Station.

MR Fares Notice

Courtesy Birmingham Reference Library

Year	Passengers No.	Receipts £	Parcels etc. £	Total £	Livestock No. trucks	Coal etc. Tons	Carted Tons	Non-Carted Tons	Mineral Class Tons	Transhipments Tons	Station Expenses £	Season Tickets No.
Whitacre												
1872	14680	912	111	1023	209	725	369	4333	1637	303	452	
1877	14197	953	181	1134	206	3228	122	1391	655	477	454	
1882	23744	1424	251	1675	142	6198	470	3410	9042	386	442	
1887	16128	1011	421	1432	188	7375	142	1361	885	319	378	21
1892	16618	993	298	1291	89	9544	126	1210	489	265	594	25
1895	16544	984	356	1340	63	12739	209	2492	1046	219	617	31
1897	16809	1013	479	1492	56	11898	222	1330	2222	235	694	35
1902	15129	992	426	1418	76	17159	173	1106	2179	261	889	42
1907	18130	1142	489	1631	70	2529	175	3326	1574	254	1138	50
1912	16237	1020	483	1503	55	4575	182	1489	6872	80		31
1917	19213	1868	362	2230	74	9659	123	1372	737	41		110
1922	19029	2436	631	3067	86	6910	125	1462	4743	32		68
Coleshill												
1872	670	14	8	22	4	1047	126	1073	680		52	
1877	327	7	11	18	1	1187	113	820	503		58	
1882	194	5	15	20	6	534	111	671	151		62	
1887	217	6	14	20	5	516	79	489	530		62	
1892	317	6	14	20	1	486	99	681	916		52	
1895	362	7	10	17		579	104	760	1124		52	
1897	408	8	14	22		597	152	883	1943		60	
1902	296	6	12	18		835	121	1083	2283		70	1
1907	423	13	5	18		1229	51	885	2098		69	
1912	209	5	10	15		1018	37	982	2516			
1917						1010	35	1017	549			
1922						1068	48	1036	728			
Hampton												
1872	1156	80	45	125	3	4093	104	1129	341	6	201	
1877	742	37	83	120	16	6262	70	1208	891	111	193	
1882	504	19	10	29	10	4542	72	1419	776	129	209	
1887	517	19	10	29	8	5539	81	1967	1760	123	64	
1892	622	21	8	29	4	4019	83	2020	1636	94	73	
1895	766	21	8	29	5	4735	87	1836	2058	89	85	
1897	521	15	10	25	2	4353	95	1585	2136	94	84	
1902	509	14	6	20	4	3884	97	1612	1944	41	96	
1907	732	68	30	98	7	4613	146	3172	2179	14	126	
1912	360	16	7	23	1	4577	112	2493	2014	4		
1917					13	4410	105	2804	1395			
1922					14	4580	76	1644	4359			

Midland Railway revenue tables up to 1922.

of power during the late nineteenth and early twentieth century was the Johnson vacuum-fitted 'M' class and his class '2' 0-6-0 tender engines. Saltley shed, MR code 3, provided most of the motive power. In the years surrounding World War II, a variety of engines found their way onto the line. Midland Compound No. 1064; Stanier freight engine class '8F' No. 48723 and numerous 'Black Fives'. 'Patriot' class No. 5526 *Morecambe and Heysham* graced the branch, and even a Beyer-Garratt crept on to it. Ivatt class '2' No. 46446 was the last engine to traverse the line, as it was used for the final track lifting.

Prior to 1880 Kirtley 4-wheeled coaches were used for passengers. Samuel Waite Johnson, who had succeeded Kirtley as Locomotive Superintendent in 1873 was the inspiration behind Thomas Clayton's superior 6-wheeled bogie coach. Upon its introduction, an arc-roof 1st/3rd brake (with smoking and non-smoking compartments) provided very comfortable accommodation until the withdrawal of passenger services.

The standard Midland Railway wagons were used for transporting goods, including a few private-owner examples.

Passenger services

An oddity of the line was the absence of a ticket machine at Coleshill, and in its later years the branch was worked by train staff without tickets at all. Up to 1845 two trains per day continued to convey through coaches to and from Euston, at which time the facility was withdrawn. From that date he local service varied from three to four passenger trains each way, although it appears that by 1877 five trains combined passenger and goods duties. It is noteworthy that the timetables of that year show the old Whitacre station still in use, and trains called at both stations in the village. Traffic must have been light, however, for in May 1877 services were cut dramatically; only one train ran each way and it did not call at the old station. It departed Whitacre at 8:30 a.m. and had returned by 10.45 a.m. This was the "Parliamentary Train". Companies were obliged to run at least one train per day, calling at all stations, conveying third-class passengers, and at a speed of 12 mph of greater. Had it not been for the prohibitive cost of raising an Act of Parliament to close the line, the branch could easily have died without ever seeing the twentieth-century.

By 1916 the turnaround of this solitary train was even quicker. Departing Whitacre at 8.10 a.m. it was back by 8.55 a.m., three-quarters of an hour later. Thus, for 23 1/4 hours out of every day the single Clayton coach languished in Whitacre sidings. Once this meagre duty was complete, and the optional goods train had run, the line was closed for the day. The last passenger train ran on Saturday 31 December 1916.

Goods traffic

The usual arrangement was for one regular return goods train per day to run, plus a conditional one, the latter depending upon the volume of traffic. The 1877 reductions saw the duties of the single daily passenger train combined with goods. Conversely, the conditional goods train had a coach attached from time to time to transport businessmen when visiting the Maxstoke estate. Coal, coke, lime, and limestone were the chief minerals carried, and the peak of freight operations at the northern end of the line was reached in 1902. A 7.00 a.m. train from Whitacre junction took coal to London.

Hampton's traffic increased steadily with the development of Wyckham Blackwell's saw mills, and by 1922 the goods yard was quite active. Trees came in by train, and timber from the mills was used by the LMS for wagon making. An inspector would oversee the delivery of one train per week for this purpose. The firm also supplied sawdust to Hams Hall once per week, and coffin boards to the north-east – 6' 6" x 18-30" x 3/4"! In the 1930s and 1940s lime was brought in, and sugar beet sent out. The last official through goods train ran on St. George's day 1930, but we shall hear of even more vital service to come in the years after war broke out.

Whitacre sidings, though, continued to be busy. Empty wagons from the three collieries on the Nuneaton line were serviced there, as were those from the Kingsbury branch collieries on occasion. Coal and goods trains were marshalled there for destinations *via* the Walsall Branch that went off at Water Orton; a daily early morning train leaving for Bushbury Sidings, Wolverhampton.

Revenue

Some idea of the reasons for reduction in services can be gleaned from the revenue tables presented on page 48. Only Whitacre was paying for itself, not surprisingly because of its key position on the Nuneaton to Birmingham line.

Hampton Station c.1931. The crossover points and dock siding were the scene of the accident in 1870.

National Railway Museum

The accident of 1903 at Whitacre. Locomotive 2344 was hauling the goods train when it hit the stopblock at the end of the siding. Passenger engine 2585 could not avoid the debris.

Warwick County Record Office

Accidents

Short though the branch was, there was no shortage of incidents. On 16 February 1848 a carriage caught fire at Hampton on a London-Birmingham train. Thirty years to the day after the Whitacre accident, another collision occurred, this time at the opposite end of the line. On 2 December 1870 a northbound train loaded with ironstone from Northampton passed the Hampton distant signal at caution. On this line "down" is towards Birmingham, and "up" towards London. The time was a little before half-past four in the afternoon. It was dark, but clear. The driver's defence was that the signal was never lowered further than caution, and so he proceeded. The sight of a red light at the rear of a passenger train ahead spurred him into urgent action, however, and he shut off steam. Despite application of the tender and guard's brakes, his speed of 26 mph was too great to avoid collision. He struck the brake-van of the train waiting in the station at a speed of five or six miles per hour. Damage to the life-guard of the engine was sustained, as well as to the lubricant and steam chest, but fortunately, neither engine nor rolling stock left the rails. The other train was the 3.15 p.m. from Leamington, having arrived at Hampton at 4.5 p.m. It should have left well before 4.20 p.m., the time of the accident. The delay was a common one, that due to difficulties in handling horses. The hounds had met at Hampton that day, so as well as the six carriages and brake-van already on the train, there were six horse-boxes waiting in the Midland station dock siding. These had to be fetched by crossing and re-crossing the up line and attaching them to the front of the train. The shunting necessary to achieve this was quite involved, so the main portion of the train was set back some distance to the south – about 100 yards – so as to clear crossover points. Having hitched up the horse boxes, the driver allowed a southbound express to pass and then ventured out across the line. He succeeded in getting the horse-boxes on to the down line, and was about to run his uncoupled engine around to the front of them by using the crossover points to the south and north. Before he could regain the up line, however, a shout alerted him to the imminent danger. Moving the horse boxes to safety, he could do no more than await the inevitable. The crash, when it came, was 887 yards within the safety of the distant-signal, but 90 yards outside the safety of the platform signal. The passenger train was shunted forwards 38 yards, and although no fatalities occurred, six passengers laid claims for injury. Evidence showed that the distant signal did not fly to "full on", and was only partly at the danger position. The driver of the ironstone train clearly did not expect to find a train that far back from the platform. The practice of time interval working (as opposed to block telegraph) at this location did not help, but the delay of 15 minutes due to managing the horse-boxes was a major factor in the accident. As a result, instructions were issued for horses to be at stations much earlier than previous practice had allowed.

The biggest accident that befell the Stonebridge Railway occurred on 18 August 1903 at Whitacre. The subsequent investigations are so exhaustive, and impressive, that the full texts of the various parts of the report are quoted. The inspecting officer was Major E. Druitt, R.E. Firstly we have a statement of events and a description of the line in the vicinity of the accident. On this line "down" is towards Hampton and Birmingham, and "up" towards Derby. It will be recalled that there are four sets of rails north of Whitacre Junction; a passenger line in each direction and an adjacent goods loop in each direction. In describing the position of signals, "behind" means ones that are encountered first.

MIDLAND RAILWAY

Railway Department, Board of Trade,
8, Richmond Terrace,
Whitehall,
London S.W.
14th September 1903.

Sir,
"I have the honour to report for the information of the Board of Trade, in compliance with the order of 22nd August, the result of my inquiry into the causes of the collision which occurred on the 18th August between a passenger train and some derailed goods waggons at Whitacre on the Midland Railway.

In this case the driver of a goods train from Birmingham to Ancoats, travelling on the up goods line between Whitacre Junction and Whitacre North Signal Boxes, ran past the outlet signal for the goods line at Whitacre North Signal Box which was at danger, and collided with the stopblock at the end of the neck, with the result that some waggons of the train were derailed and fouled the up passenger line just as a special passenger train from Bristol to Hellifield was passing on that line.

The engine of the passenger train was partially derailed, and all the carriages damaged by contact with the derailed waggons.

Nine passengers complained of injuries.

The passenger train consisted of a four-

51

wheels-coupled bogie engine with a six-wheeled tender running chimney first, fitted with a steam brake working blocks on the four coupled wheels and six tender wheels, in conjunction with the vacuum brake on the vehicles.

The goods train consisted of a six-wheels-coupled engine and six-wheeled tender with the steam brake working blocks on all wheels of the engine and tender. The blocks on the tender could also be applied by hand. Behind the engine were nineteen loaded waggons, four empty waggons, and a ten-ton brake van.

The brakes of both trains are stated to have been in good order.

The accident occurred at 1.49 a.m. on a wet and dark night.

Details of the damage to permanent way and rolling stock are given in the Appendix.

Description.

Approaching Whitacre Junction from Birmingham the passenger lines run approximately from north-west to south-east, but at either end of the platforms are sharp curves, so that a little beyond the station they run from south to north, the up line being on the west side of the down line. Forty yards beyond the north end of the up platform the up goods line commences by a pair of facing points in the up Derby passenger line, and it runs parallel to this line (with a 10-foot space between the two) to Whitacre North Signal Box, where the goods line joins the passenger line again, and there is a short over-run of 40 yards, ending in a stopblock.

The length of this up goods loop is about 1,320 yards. The signalling arrangements are complete in every respect.

At the north end of the up platform are the usual starting signals for the three lines diverging there, viz., the up line to Leicester, the up passenger line to Derby, and the up goods line to Derby. These three signals are on brackets, the signal for the up goods line being to the left, and lower than the up Derby passenger line.

Two hundred and twenty yards behind the above signals are a similar bunch of up home signals, one for each of the above-mentioned lines, and some distance behind these are three up distant signals relating to the same lines. There is a starting signal for the up passenger line to Derby, situated in the 10-foot space between the up passenger and up goods line, so that it is on the left of the passenger and on the right of the goods line.

The signals at Whitacre North Signal Box consist of a single home signal for the up passenger line opposite the signal box protecting the junction of the goods and passenger lines, situated in the 10-foot space between the two lines, and of an outlet signal for the goods line, situated on the left side of that line, just at the facing trap points leading out on to the passenger line.

There is also an up main line starting signal 360 yards ahead of the home signal.

The home signal is 70 yards behind the goods line outlet signal.

The gradients are quite easy, being 1 in 407 and 1 in 543 between Whitacre Junction and Whitacre North Signal Boxes."

Next we have the statements from all nine individuals concerned. They were: Charles Ward, signalman at Whitacre Junction. Sam Butler, signalman at Whitacre North. Arthur John Collis, driver of the goods train; Edward William Randall, his fireman; Jesse Morley, his guard. George James Herbert Hawkins, driver of the passenger train; William Insley, his fireman; James Turner, his guard; David Taylor, under-guard to Turner. All gave competent, lucid accounts of events leading up to the collision. Their *average* length of service was no less than 21 years. The most telling testimony is that of driver Collis.

Evidence.

"*Arthur John Collis*, driver, states: I have been in the service 25 years, and have been a driver 12 years. I signed on duty at 9.15 p.m. on the 17th August, to work till 7.30 a.m. on the 18th with the 10.40 p.m. goods train from Birmingham Central to Ancoats. I had then been off duty 39 hours, after performing nine hours work. I am well aquainted with the road throughout, and have travelled over it for about 12 years. My engine was a six-wheeled-coupled goods engine with six-wheeled tender, fitted with the steam brake, and with brake blocks to all wheels of the engine and tender and with the hand brake on the tender wheels. The brake was in good working order. When I approached Whitacre Junction distant signals they were at danger and I shut off steam in preparedness for passing them. Approaching the Whitacre Junction home signals I saw one green light which I took to be that for the main line, but did not observe the other two, which I account for by reason of the steam and smoke from my engine obscuring the view, as it was raining very heavily, and the steam damped down. I do not know which signal of the three was showing a green light, but I was prepared to stop at the directing signals, and knew that any one of the three home signals would admit to the directing signals. When approaching the three directing signals at Whitacre Junction I saw one light, which was a green one, and I proceeded on the assumption that it was the up passenger line directing signal, and that I was required to run upon the up passenger line. I attribute my inability to see the other two directing signals to the same cause that prevented me from seeing the home signal. After passing the directing signals, I drew the rear of the train clear of the Junction, and then stopped, my engine at this time being about 60 or 70 yards on the Junction side of the up passenger line starting signal. I stopped for that signal to be lowered, as I was still under the impression that I was on the up passenger line. After standing, as I think, about three or four minutes I saw the starting signal for the up passenger line, worked from Whitacre Junction, lowered, and the North Box distant signal, which is on the same post, also taken off. I then proceeded, and approaching Whitacre North Box home signal I believe I was running at about 15 or 18 miles per hour, and when I sighted that signal it was off, as was also the North Box starting signal applying to the passenger line. Still supposing that I was on the up passenger line, I applied more steam, and passed Whitacre North Box at about 18 miles per hour, and should be travelling at that speed when I struck the buffer stops. I account for not discovering that my train was passing Whitacre Junction starting signal on the goods line side of it by the fact that I did not notice as I passed it, being at the time engaged in looking at my watch. I do not remember seeing the North Box home signal when I passed it, as I had seen it "off" when I passed the up starting signal. I did not discover anything amiss until my engine actually struck the stopblock. I did not, therefore, shout, reverse my engine, or whistle for the Guard's brake before running into the stopblock. I did not observe that the home signal and starting signal, worked from Whitacre North Box, were reversed. I was handling the regulator myself. My fireman was firing when approaching Whitacre Junction, but when I drew his attention to the fact that the signal was at danger, he stopped doing so, but as two or three lumps of coal had fallen on the footplate, he commenced to pick them up. I was on the footplate at the time the collision happened. The only injury which I sustained, as the result of the accident, was a slight shock."

Collis's fireman Randall confirmed his driver's version of events, although Morley, the guard, estimated their impact speed at nearer 30 mph. Signalman Butler, on seeing Collis pass his box at speed, attempted to avert a disaster by immediately throwing all his signals to danger, but the passenger train was already upon the scene. Hawkins and Insley never saw the goods train ahead of them. Fortunately, none of the enginemen or guards received serious injury, but a tremendous amount of debris was created when the passenger train hit the derailed wagons. Finally, the inspector summed up as follows.

Conclusion.

"The cause of this collision is driver Collis's failure to observe the correct signals, and his mistaking the line upon which his train was travelling.. He states that he did not feel his engine take the points, which is probable, as the turn is a gentle one and he was travelling at a very low speed. The stopblock was of course demolished, the engine ran off the end of the line, and the nine wagons next to the engine were broken up and fouled the up passenger line. The special passenger train hit the wreckage a few seconds later, and the engine was partially derailed, but none of the vehicles left the road. Making every allowance for the rough night and other circumstances, I consider driver Collis did not pay sufficient attention to his duties, and must be held responsible for the collision. He is a man with an excellent record, and had been on duty four hours and a-half at the time of the collision. The men on the passenger engine had all signals off for them, and had no chance of avoiding the collision."

Major E. Druitt, R.E.

Attached to the report was a very detailed Appendix listing the damage to engines and vehicles. The goods locomotive, No. 2344 was a wreck, and its tender suffered badly. The passenger engine No. 2585 received mainly superficial damage, and its tender escaped with just a slightly bent tool box lid. The vehicles of the passenger train were badly spoiled on their left hand side, but it was the goods wagons that took the main brunt of the devastation. Eight were completely broken up, with five more sustaining serious damage. The track bed itself was heavily ripped up. The toll was one iron stop, 69 50lb chairs, 556 treenails, 120 spikes and two side rail bolts broken, 278 sleepers more or less damaged. It was quite a mess.

Veritas Vincit would have had a field day. Let us close this chapter of woe with some observations from *Punch*. Accidents were always news, but the press was becoming increasingly cynical when assessing statements put out by company officials in respect of the latest calamity on their lines.

A GLOSSARY TO RAILWAY PHRASES

"The passengers were severely shaken." Hundreds of people barely escaped with their lives.

"No casualty is reported." The representative of the press not having as yet arrived on the spot where the accident took place.

"The accident was not serious." Only half-a-dozen railway officials killed and wounded.

"The accident was caused by unavoidable circumstances." New words for gross carelessness and reckless stupidity.

"The express was dispatched at its usual hour." The train was hurriedly started off some forty minutes late.

"The pointsman was at his post." And had been there for the last eighteen hours.

"The accident is to be much regretted." A vision of passengers obtaining heavy damages awarded them by sympathetic juries of their countrymen.

"The alteration, recommended at the inquest, was on the point of being made at the very time the accident happened." The danger, although fully appreciated for years, had been considered unworthy of the expense that its removal would entail, until a public exposure rendered the outlay necessary.

"Hasty legislation is to be deprecated." As the directors have no wish to render themselves liable to be tried for manslaughter.

"An accident of this character is not likely to occur again." Until the next time! – *Punch*.

MIDLAND RAILWAY.

THE MIDLAND RAILWAY CO.

HAVE VACANCIES FOR A NUMBER OF

STEADY MEN

QUALIFIED TO ACT AS

GOODS GUARDS,

And others having Railway experience, who are willing to be trained for such duties.

The Conditions of Service for Goods' Guards are as follows :—
Under-Guards in the Country, 20s. per Week, with Clothing.
"   in London, 23s.   "   "
Head-Guards, from 24s. to 30s. per week, with Clothing.

When the Men are required to sleep from home, 2s. per night in the country, and 3s. per night in London is allowed for Lodging expenses.

The Men will work either on the Time System or on the Trip System, as may be required by the Company.

When working on the Time System, 66 hours to constitute a Week's work; all Overtime to be paid for at the rate of 11 hours per day.

The payments for men working on the Trip System, are carefully calculated upon the average time occupied by each Trip.

If the Trains are unavoidably delayed by circumstances beyond the Guard's control, an allowance will be made for the extra time.

The Men to give and receive a Fortnight's Notice before leaving the Company's Service.

Application to be made to

Mr. E. M. NEEDHAM,

SUPERINTENDENT of the LINE,
MIDLAND RAILWAY, DERBY.

Derby, Jan. 4th, 1879.   **JAMES ALLPORT**, General-Manager.

Bemrose and Sons, Printers, London and Derby.

Employment notice 1879

54

Rollason's yard in 1936.

Phil and Nancy Rollason

Phil and Charles Rollason celebrate their firm's centenary in 1984.

Phil and Nancy Rollason

The daily Whitacre – Hampton goods train approaches Bridge 18 south of Packington Ford in 1902. A Johnson 0-6-0 is in charge as usual.

Bridge 22, the Chester Road crossing c.1921. A wagon can be seen in Packington siding to the left.

Hampton in 1916. The daily passenger train pauses on its way past the MR signal box. It was heading for the 'new' station, some half mile to the south.

Courtesy P E B Butler

Hampton Station c.1931. Looking towards the goods yard, the branch diverged to the right. The platform signal was still in use for goods, and the LMS signal box is seen on the left.

National Railway Museum

Hampton station in November 1935.

Courtesy Mike Bryant

Hampton Station c.1937. Disused but still attractive. An unusual view taken from the down main line. The bay windows were double glazed.

National Railway Museum

The former B&DJR engine shed in 1931.

National Railway Museum

Wyckham Blackwell's yard in 1932

Courtesy W D Butler

Wyckham Blackwell and nieces at 'The Hut' c.1930

W D Butler (left) and his father F S Butler (right). Two generations that carried the firm of Wyckam Blackwell to its centenary in 1984.

CHAPTER EIGHT

For Queen and Country

Royalty

For royal visitors, the Stonebridge Railway has a record that is perhaps unequalled in branch line history. The list is impressive. From Queen Victoria to Queen Elizabeth II, every generation of royalty has graced this little line in one way or another. The 1843 visit of Queen Victoria was not the only time that she travelled upon it. On 29/30 September 1849 her Majesty journeyed from Balmoral *via* Derby and Birmingham to Gosport, staying overnight at the *Midland Hotel*, Derby. Her final destination was Osborne House on the Isle of Wight. Her train could have run along the direct line into Birmingham, but that arrangement would have necessitated shunting using the lift in order to gain access to The Birmingham and Gloucester line. Far too undignified! Her party arrived at Hampton on a wet Saturday morning at 9.26 a.m. Continuing towards Birmingham, the train arrived there twenty minutes later. Matthew Kirtley again drove her train, from Normanton to Derby at least, and probably to Hampton as well.

2 November 1874 was the date of a visit to Packington Hall by Edward, Prince of Wales, and Princess Alexandra, as guests of the seventh Earl of Aylesford. They were to pay official visits to the cities of Birmingham and Coventry over the next few days. *Sojourns* to country estates such as Packington were frequent by the future King Edward VII at this time, and he arrived at Hampton station in the evening, transferring to waiting carriages for the journey to the Hall. He was met by Lord Aylesford and various railway officials. Hampton station was richly decorated for the occasion under the guidance of Mr. Sutton, traffic superintendent of the LNWR. The *Coleshill Chronicle* notices these preparations well:

"A triumphal arch has been erected, and a large number of coloured lamps was hung among the trees on either side of the carriage leading up to the hall. The road from the hall to Hampton station was diversified as to scenery, and positively charming in its autumn garb. There is, however, an almost entire absence of houses along the route, and this will account for little decoration having been made. At the Stonebridge Inn some pretty illuminations were prepared, and this was the sole break to the rather lonely journey of over three miles. At the railway station, however, the preparations were extensive, appropriate, and useful. Ordinary passengers must have had to submit to straits on Monday, for the station was almost closed to them. Everyone, stationmaster included, was busy, not in creating decorations, but in converting the somewhat bare and desolate-looking station into a fitting place of reception for Royalty. Inspector Squires, of Birmingham, was present, with a large staff of assistants, carrying out the arrangements. The station itself is somewhat awkwardly situated, as passengers arriving from London not only have to cross the main line, but after climbing over a platform have to cross a second line, which is in fact the old Midland Railway from Hampton to Derby. To obviate this inconvenience, it was arranged that the Royal train should run into the station and be shunted back on to this old Derby line. Here a temporary platform was erected to be on a level with the floors of the railway carriages. The whole of this platform, together with the balustrade at the side, was covered with rich velvet pile crimson carpet, the top of the balustrades being relieved by a broad strip of bright scarlet cloth. Lamps were erected on each side of the platform. The interior of the station building was completely draped with bands of white and scarlet cloth, and outside a small platform was barricaded off to allow of the Royal party reaching their carriages without interruption."

Their saloon carriages left London at 3.00 p.m., attached to a normal express train. At Rugby a special train was formed for the journey to Hampton. Again, we let the *Coleshill Chronicle* pick up the tale:

"For two or three hours before the time announced for the arrival of the train, visitors commenced to congregate around Hampton Station. Many of them appeared to have come from some distance, and a long string of vehicles was soon arranged in the vicinity of

Queen Victoria's Royal Train at Cheltenham in 1849.

5526 'Morecambe and Heysham' had just been shopped out in February 1938 following an overhaul. On 10 March 1938 it hauled the Royal Train of King George VI off the branch from Hampton Midland station.

the station. Later on the children of the Hampton Parish School arrived in wagons with their Sunday school banners. The platforms of the station were kept clear with the exception of the favoured few, who had received tickets from the superintendents of the line. The evening was not a very favourable one – the atmosphere being cold and raw, and a slight fog prevailing. The expectant visitors, however, kept their courage warm by rehearsing loyal songs, in which the school children joined heartily. In order to prevent the possibility of any mishap, plate layers, with hand lamps, were posted along the line, Londonwards, for more than half a mile from the station; and, indeed, every possible preparation seemed to have been made. Shortly after five o' clock the Earl of Aylesford accompanied by Colonel Owen Williams and Colonel Finch, arrived at the station, and a long train of carriages from the Hall was placed in readiness. Precisely at 5.40, the time announced for the arrival, the signal was given, and the Royal train was in sight, and in a few minutes it slowly drew up to the station and backed into the siding, as arranged. Whilst this operation was being performed the Prince of Wales was descried at the window, waving his hand to the Earl of Aylesford, and the spectators at once set up a hearty cheer. On the Prince, with the Princess alighting, they exchanged warm greetings with the Earl of Aylesford, and at once hurried off, amid the continued cheers of the spectators, through the station to the carriages. The park, indeed, presented a scene of unwonted splendour. As the Royal party alighted at the door of the hall amid the cheers of the assembled tenantry, the band of the Warwickshire Yeomanry Cavalry was playing "God bless the Prince of Wales." A maroon, with a sudden explosion shot whirling into the air, and instantaneously a large portion of the park in front of the hall was brilliantly illuminated with delicately tinted fires. At the same instant also frames of Roman Candles which had been placed amongst the trees were ignited, and hundreds of coloured stars were seen flying in all directions. Balloons, too, bearing magnesium lights, were sent up, and these must have been visible for many miles around. The spectacle, on the whole, was a gorgeous one, and his Royal Highness the Prince of Wales, who stood in front of the hall to witness it, frequently expressed his admiration."

This grand occasion was remembered in 1935 by a long time resident of Hampton, Mrs. King, the postmistress. She was born in 1862 and recalled the festivities thus:

"I was at school and we all went to the station and stood in wagons, singing "God Bless The Prince of Wales". What impressed me most I think were the Chinese servants with pigtails down their backs, we could not understand why their hair was done like that; there were also Indian servants with turbans. The next morning we went on to the Coventry Road to see them go to Birmingham; they stopped while we sang again, and of course we were very excited."

On 22 May 1919 Queen Mary visited Maxstoke Castle, arriving by royal Daimler, and possibly crossing the line in Maxstoke Lane at the site of Coleshill station.

About 1935, it is reputed, a gentleman walking on the line at Whitacre approached a local horse breeder and introduced himself as the Prince Of Wales. If true, this would be the future King Edward VIII, but in the years leading up to World War II it was not unknown for false trails to be laid where Royalty was concerned, and so this tale should be treated with caution.

What is certain is the visit of his brother King George VI on 10 March 1938. In the years leading up to World War II, the efforts to arm the country were intense, especially in the Midlands. The King wished to see for himself how these preparations were progressing, and arrangements were made for a tour of factories in the Birmingham and Coventry area. It was originally planned to stable his train overnight on the Hampton branch, but when this fact became public knowledge arrangements were prudently changed.

His train was eventually stabled in Barnt Green sidings. After spending the Wednesday night there he toured the Austin factory on Thursday morning, during which time his train was conveyed to Hampton Midland Station sidings by "Compound" class engine No. 1014. The King arrived there by road after also visiting the Rover factory. He was met by stationmaster Wilson and took luncheon on board, departing at 1.30 p.m. His train was hauled off the branch by "Patriot" class engine No. 5526 *Morecambe and Heysham* to Tile Hill. From there he toured the Humber and Standard works before returning to London.

Prior to the introduction of the Queen's Flight in the early 1950s, royalty travelled regularly by train. During and immediately after World War II King George VI and Queen Elizabeth the Queen Mother visited the Midlands on a number of occasions. A secluded, well covered cutting between Maxstoke and Whitacre afforded very good shelter from air attacks, and was used as a stabling point for the royal train. The young Princess Elizabeth accompanied them on occasion. Details are sketchy due to the nature of the period, but Sir William Dugdale, through whose land the line ran, assures the author of the exactness of this arrangement.

On 20 February 1976 The Duke of Edinburgh stayed overnight in the royal train at Whitacre Junction in the sidings of the old branch line. He was opening a new extension to the nearby Shustoke Reservoir.

Finally, on 24 November 1983 Charles, Prince of Wales, carried out an inspection at Whittington Barracks, and he too, used the junction as an overnight resting place.

World Wars

Very little is known of events on the railway during the Great War of 1914 – 1918, although some of the rails from the branch were sent to what was then Mesopotamia as part of the war effort. World War II, however, was a different matter. The Stonebridge Railway gave sterling service in a number of ways.

From the start of the war, the sheltered cuttings near to Coleshill offered a safe haven for ammunition trains, although not many residents knew of their existence at the time. An urgent need existed for sand in the construction of aerodrome runways. Sand was, and still is, an abundant feature of Warwickshire soil. Bannerley pits at Packington proved a major source of this material, and to aid its transport a small concrete loading platform was built adjacent to the line at Packington ford in 1940. This enabled the sand to be tipped from dumper trucks directly into waiting wagons. Great Bowden, in Northamptonshire, was just one aerodrome to benefit from this arrangement. A special train, leaving Hampton-in-Arden at 6.22 p.m. on Mondays, Wednesdays and Fridays, was booked to work this traffic. The motive power was usually a Fowler '4F' 0-6-0 tender engine, taking the train at least as far as Coventry, but it was not unknown for a class '5' locomotive to substitute for this duty. On at least one occasion a 'Black Five' made it up the line as far as Little Packington.

The two major road bridges at Bickenhill were strengthened at this time. Just as well, for two land mines were dropped nearby. At the Hampton end a Royal Artillery 4.7" mobile gun was used for anti-aircraft purposes. An engine was attached for propelling it up and down the line. Also at Hampton was based a secret Air Ministry control centre. Some of the officers were billeted in the village, and the remains of the concrete foundations of the buildings can be seen alongside the track bed in Old Station Road today.

ARP exercises were carried out on the line near to Castle Farm, Maxstoke. The redundant goods siding there was lifted around 1943 and an old 6-wheeled coach placed upon two short lengths of line, with some timber huts being erected alongside. Specially installed points and signalling equipment were dynamited, and sprayed with mustard gas. The repair crews were then invited to attend to matters.

All through the war the movement of goods and men took priority on the railways. Often, the sidings at Washwood Heath and Lawley Street simply could not cope with the traffic. The trains had to go somewhere else and on occasions up to six trains were propelled down the branch at Whitacre for stabling. This often necessitated laborious shunting when a particular load was required urgently.

From 1935 onwards the line had been used a repository for crippled wagons, and after the war ended the lines of broken down trucks grew lengthier as time went on until eventually 180 of them were hauled off the branch by a Beyer-Garratt locomotive. It is likely that mineral trains continued to use the line up to 1946.

There is a strong belief that a passenger train did in fact traverse the whole of the branch during the war due to bombing around the Lea Hall area. Apparently the line here was impassable so a Birmingham to Coventry train went via Whitacre and Hampton in order to avoid the obstacle. It would have had to cross the dilapidated timber river bridges very gingerly indeed! In wartime of course, anything is possible.

To end this chapter on a happier note, in around 1950 a camping coach was stored briefly at the Coleshill end of Whitacre sidings. It must have made light relief from the ammunition trains. Certainly the Stonebridge Railway did its fair share of work in those dark days, and its contribution was a noble one. Sadly, though, the ending of the war also hastened the demise of the branch line. There was to be no respite. Well, perhaps just a little.

E.R.O. 53360/3.

London Midland and Scottish Railway Company.

NOTICE OF

ROYAL SPECIAL TRAINS

LONDON (Euston) to BARNT GREEN

Wednesday Night, March 9th

and

Thursday Morning, March 10th

BARNT GREEN to COFTON GROUND FRAME

HAMPTON (Mid.) to TILE HILL

COVENTRY to LONDON (Euston)

Thursday, March 10th

1938

TIME TABLE.

WEDNESDAY, MARCH 9TH, 1938.

MILES				
				p.m.
—	**EUSTON** . . . dep.			11.10
				a.m.
82½	Rugby . . . . pass			12.45
112¾	Birmingham . . . { arr.			1.25
	{ dep.			1.27
123¼	**BARNT GREEN** . . arr.			1.52
				(THURSDAY)

THURSDAY, MARCH 10TH, 1938.

			a.m.
—	**BARNT GREEN** . . dep.		9.50
1½	**COFTON FACTORY** . arr.		10. 0
			p.m.
—	**HAMPTON** . . . dep.		1.30
5¾	**TILE HILL** . . . arr.		1.45
			p.m.
—	**COVENTRY** . . . dep.		5. 0
11½	Rugby . . . . pass		5.14
62¼	Tring . . . . ,,		6. 2
94	**EUSTON** . . . arr.		6.35

LONDON MIDLAND AND SCOTTISH RAILWAY COMPANY.

WEDNESDAY NIGHT, MARCH 9th, and THURSDAY MORNING, MARCH 10th, 1938
ROYAL SPECIAL TRAIN—LONDON (Euston) TO BARNT GREEN.

Miles.			
			p.m.
—	EUSTON (No. 6 Platform)... ... . dep.		11 10
5½	Willesden Junction ... ... pass		11 20
17½	Watford Junction ... ... ,,		11 34
31¾	Tring ... ... ,,		11 51
			a.m.
46¾	Bletchley ... ... ,,		12 6
60	Roade ... ... ,,		12 20
62¾	Blisworth ... ... ,,		12 23
82½	Rugby (Down Through Line) ... ... ,,		12 45
94	Coventry ... ... ,,		1 1
112¾	BIRMINGHAM (No. 6-4 Down Platform) ... { arr. { dep.		1 25 / 1 27
116	Selly Oak ... ... pass		1 37
118	King's Norton ... ... ,,		1 42
123¼	BARNT GREEN ... ... arr.		1 52

The Royal Train will travel on the Down Main, Passenger or Fast Line (where more than one line exists), unless shown otherwise below:—

EUSTON.—The Royal Train will start from No. 6 Platform.

RUGBY.—The Royal Train will travel over the Down Birmingham Line from Rugby No. 5 to No. 7 Signal-box.

BIRMINGHAM.—The Royal Train will arrive at No. 6-4 Down Platform. It must come to a stand at the Platform starting signal where the Enginemen and Guard will be changed.

BARNT GREEN.—The Royal Train will run to the Down Redditch platform line. It must come to a stand with the cab of the engine opposite a point at which a man will be stationed exhibiting a hand signal. The train will then be drawn from the Down Redditch platform line through the siding next adjoining the Down Slow line and come to a stand with the cab of the engine opposite a point at which a man will be stationed exhibiting a hand signal. It will afterwards be drawn into the Coal Yard Road where it must come to a stand with the cab of the engine opposite a point at which a man will be stationed exhibiting a hand signal.

The following trains to be altered as shown:—

11. 5 p.m. "Q" Euston to Edinburgh, if run, to follow the Royal Train.

10.40 p.m. Parcels, Euston to Manchester, to follow the Royal Train from Willesden.

12.22 a.m. Light Engine, Rugby to Coventry, to follow the Royal Train.

1.20 a.m. Empty Stock, Vauxhall to Birmingham, to leave at 1.25 a.m.

THURSDAY, MARCH 10th, 1938.

ROYAL SPECIAL TRAIN—BARNT GREEN TO COFTON GROUND FRAME.

Miles.			
			a.m.
—	BARNT GREEN ... ... dep.		9 50
1½	COFTON GROUND FRAME ... ... arr.		10 0

BARNT GREEN.—The Royal Train will be drawn from the Coal Yard Road direct to the Up Slow Line at Barnt Green.

COFTON GROUND FRAME.—The Royal Train will arrive Cofton Ground Frame on the Up Slow Line, and must come to a stand with the cab of the engine opposite a point at which a man will be stationed exhibiting a hand signal.

The following trains to be altered as shown:—

7.42 a.m. Bristol to Sheffield to be held at Blackwell until the Royal Train has left Barnt Green.

ROYAL SPECIAL TRAIN—HAMPTON (Mid.) TO TILE HILL.

Miles.			
			p.m.
—	HAMPTON (Mid.) ... ... dep.		1 30
5¾	TILE HILL ... ... arr.		1 45

HAMPTON (Mid.).—The Royal Train will start from the old Midland platform line. No train or engine (except the engines concerned in the movement of the Royal Train) must be allowed on the Branch Line at the Hampton end from 11.0 a.m. until after departure of the Royal Train.

TILE HILL.—The Royal Train must come to a stand with the cab of the engine opposite a point at which a man will be stationed exhibiting a hand signal.

The following trains to be altered as shown:—

1 3 p.m. Birmingham to Coventry to depart Stechford 1.30 p.m. and must not leave Marston Green until the Royal Train has passed Hampton-in-Arden.

MP ¾ at Blyth End in March 1991. Fully restored 'in situ' by the author. The site of numerous Royal visits.

R N Waring

MP ½ near to the Coleshill Road, in March 1991.

R N Waring

GWR King Class 4-6-0 N° 6024 King Edward I. Seen here in the 1930s at Westbury, this restored engine ran via Whitacre Junction on 24 January 1991. Another Royal visitor!

National Railway Museum

Maxstoke crossing c.1949. An air of post-war finality pervades the scene.

National Railway Museum

CHAPTER NINE

Decline and closure

Death throes

Decline set in very early, as we have seen. In 1842 the line became a true branch. Up to then it had been a double track main line, no less. It suffered further ignominy in 1843 by losing one set of metals. And so, after only 4 years of operation, it effectively became a backwater. From 1845 to 1877 it staggered on, with a mere handful of trains each day. For the next forty years the line supported but a single passenger train and the minimum of goods trains. The withdrawal of passenger services on 1 January 1917 made Coleshill station virtually redundant. The stationmaster's duties were then restricted to servicing the crossing gates when the daily goods train passed through.

Hampton suffered a similar fate, but at least it had small industry close by. All accounts at this time note the desolate nature of the station itself, however. On 24 April 1930 the through goods trains ran no more, and the line from Maxstoke to Hampton was closed as an economy measure. From then on the line was used for the storage of wagons that had no further use in life. By 22 September of that year the Hampton end was reduced to a siding.

One of the timber bridges halfway along the line failed on 12 January 1935, and that effectively sealed the fate of the branch for ever. A section of track was lifted on either side of the bridge and laid across the rails. For the first time the line was split.

In 1936 the stationmaster of Maxstoke, Mr. Leary, retired, never having issued a ticket to bear that station's name. 1937 saw the removal of the Hampton fixed distant and home signals, but oddly enough those at Maxstoke received new spectacles and a fresh coat of paint. About this time Maxstoke station was sold to Mr. Leary. Goods from Maxstoke to Whitacre ceased on 1 May 1939, at which time the level crossing gates at Maxstoke were padlocked. The adjacent coal wharf also closed.

On 15 September 1942 the line was cut 870 yards north of the failed bridge, and a stop block erected. A year later another timber bridge failed. Wagon storage south of Maxstoke ceased, and on 7 September 1943 a protecting stop block was provided 50 yards north of Maxstoke Crossing.

The unkindest acts started on 26 November 1951. The track at the northern end was lifted, leaving just a one and a-half mile section for use as a siding. At least a small section of it close to Whitacre Junction was still double track though, despite the economies of 1843. In January 1952 the Chester Road was widened, during which time the bridge over the line was filled in. From 1951 track lifting started in earnest throughout the length of the line. Some at the Hampton end was done first, then the timber bridges were dismantled and the centre portion of the track removed, the contractors probably working towards Whitacre. Conflicting accounts exist as to when the centre portion was completely taken up – the official records show July to October 1952, but a local resident at Coleshill insists that it was July to August 1953. It is possible that there were two separate operations, working in different directions due to the problem of the river crossings. All that was left was a 3/4 mile section at each end for use as sidings.

Just prior to this the old Midland signal box frames and levers were still in place at Hampton, and they were probably removed at the same time as the main track. The box itself was long gone. On 23 March 1958 Whitacre North signal box closed.

1960 was a year of sadness at Maxstoke. First Mrs. Leary the wife of the stationmaster died a year after reaching her century. The old station building had always been basic in its facilities, and in the September it was condemned by the local authority. Various minor repairs were carried out, but to no avail. In November 1961 Mr. & Mrs. Leary's daughter Dorothy, the remaining occupant of the station, was rehoused. In January 1962 a local resident offered to buy the station from British Rail, and whilst they were prepared to accede to the request, the local authority was adamant. Maxstoke had to go. What happened next assured its fate. Whilst the building lay empty, it was a target for vandals, and in the February severe fire damage was caused to the interior. Even a piano was burned, with sheets of music

North of Bridge 17 at Packington Ford c.1949. Todd's Rough is to the left background. The line of crippled wagons grew to number 180.

National Railway Museum

Maxstoke station in 1962, soon to be abandoned.

Colin Brookes

72

Bridge 16 in 1920, facing Whitacre. This bridge failed in 1935, effectively severing the line.

Courtesy R S Carpenter

Bridge 16 in 1948 following its failure some 13 years earlier. The parapet has gone and the track lifted either side.

Eric S Tonks

scattered upon the surrounding farmland. On 6 March 1962 the demolition order was issued, and by 16 May it had gone. Mr. Whittaker of Marston Green carried out the job for £45.

By 1965 not much was left of the branch. The sidings in Blackwell's yard at Hampton had been lifted in 1963/4. The bridge in Old Station Road was demolished too, and the cutting to the north was filled in as far as the Coventry Road. On 4 January 1965, rather belatedly, Hampton was officially closed to goods. Whitacre followed suit on 1 March.

Three years later Whitacre suffered even greater indignity. Despite much opposition from the hundred or so daily users of the station, it was closed to passengers on 3 March 1968, and demolished soon afterwards. There was a bright spot, however. The up goods line north of the station was converted into an engineer's siding, and a permanent way maintenance depot was established on the site soon afterwards. In 1969, on 10 August both Whitacre signal boxes were demolished. The siding at Whitacre was reduced to 300 yards on 12 December 1970, and subsequently cut back to its point of origin at the junction. The ground frame remains, however, alongside milepost 0. On 4 April 1982 the up goods line at Whitacre North was taken out of use. It was lifted quite recently.

The Stonebridge Railway has taken a long time to die, and yet part of it lives on.

The end of the line?

It will be remembered that the original route of the Stonebridge Railway as defined in its Act of Parliament was from Whitacre to Hampton. Where in Whitacre? Near to the *Railway Inn*. In fact adjacent to the village hall. Three-quarters of a mile north of Whitacre Junction. The stretch of track heading north from the junction still exists. It has been used over the years for the delivery of coal to Hams Hall power station. New sleepers adorn the track side at the time of writing. Plans have been passed to develop a freight terminal on the site of the now demolished power station. What then, does the future hold for the remnants of our little railway? A lot more trains, that's for certain!

A Stroll Through History

To complete the story of *The Stonebridge Railway*, we take a walk down the line from Whitacre to Hampton, recalling bygone days as the route is described. The Ordnance Survey maps of 1903 provide nostalgic companions on our explorations. Most of the land is inaccessible, but locations allowing of public access are indicated where appropriate. The writer would stress that in the absence of such specific reference to public access, it must be assumed that the ground is private.

Whitacre Heath to Whitacre Junction.

We start at *The Swan Inn*. Behind it, and to the east of the superb sandstone bridge No. 97, a public footpath runs southwards alongside the line, which is still in use. Looking across it we observe the site of the 1903 crash. Near to allotments at a gap in the cottages can be seen the site of the 1842 station, and a pile of rubble – the remains of Whitacre North signal box. On a Saturday morning in 1949 Eric Toone, the signalman, watched Beyer-Garratt 47979 drop its water scoop on the crossover and get stuck solid. Burning the scoop off was the only solution! It is here that *The Stonebridge Railway* started. *The Railway Inn* lies opposite the position of the station.

From a footbridge, bridge 97A, an excellent view of the line can be gained. In rough pasture to the south, the 1842 Birmingham line diverged to the west. The map shows its commencement clearly. A Midland Railway boundary post survives alongside the path close to the base of the bridge. An old signal indicator post has also somehow been left undisturbed. At the point where the lane was crossed by the Birmingham line a level crossing existed, and maybe in later years, even a bridge.

The footpath deviates here, the line continuing due south. When the path returns another boundary post can be seen close by as we approach bridge 98. The path now runs alongside a coppice adjacent to the track as Whitacre Junction is neared. 100 yards to the south of the bridge on the west side of the line S.B. is marked on the map. This must refer to the site of an old junction box, maybe even the very first, pre-1899 one. Old timber supports of some sort can clearly be discerned. It was along this section that the derailment of 1840 occurred.

Whitacre Junction.

The path now crosses the Nuneaton line and continues into fields away from the line. An extensive layout masks the early routes. No sign now of the large island platform upon which the large station once stood. No cows, either, to stray onto the adjacent line and squeeze a wagon off the tracks. The 1839 track shows on the map as a pair of parallel lines from *Whitacre Junction* to the bottom of the sheet. The 1864 revision is recorded by the curving tracks to the west. MP 0 signifies the commencement of the old branch, but also marks the limit of present-day operations on

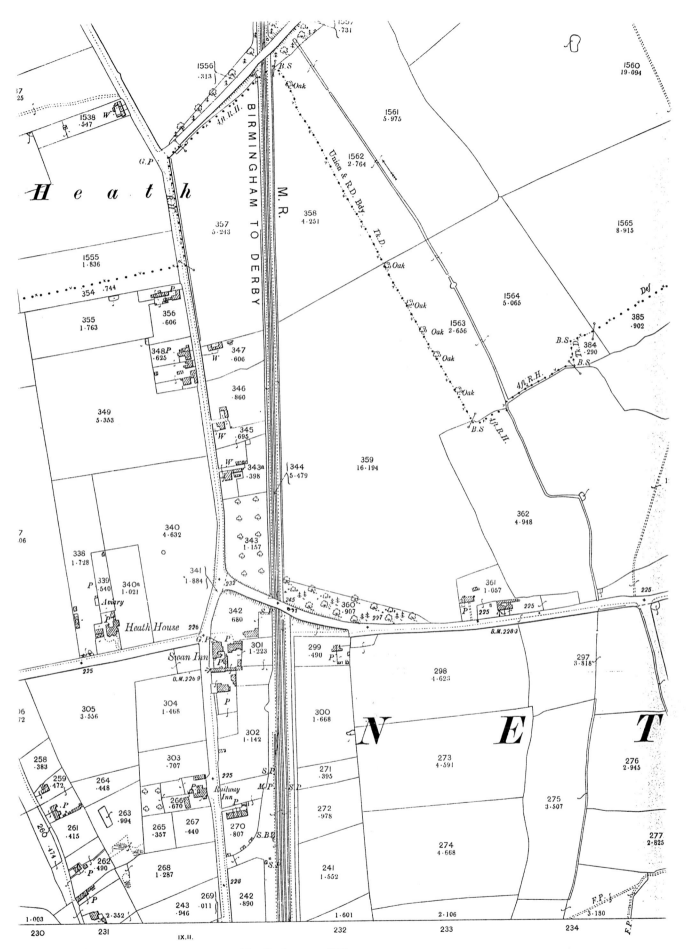

H e a t h

N   E   T

BIRMINGHAM TO DERBY M.R.

1538 .547 W

1555 1.836

354 .744

355 1.763

356 .606

348P .625

357 5.243

358 4.251

1556 .313

B.S

Oak

1561 5.975

1562 2.764

Union & R.D. Bdy. Tk.D.

1560 19.094

1565 8.915

1564 5.065

1563 2.656

Oak

Oak

Oak

Oak

Oak

Def

385 .902

384 .290

B.S

B.S

B.S

349 5.353

346 .860

347 .606

345 .695

343a .398

344 5.479

359 16.194

362 4.948

340 4.632

343 1.157

338 1.728

339 .540

340a 1.021

341 1.884

232

342 680

Aviary

Heath House 226

361 1.057

P 225

225

225

B.M.228.3

297 3.818

Swan Inn

G.P

B.M.226.9

301 1.223

299 .490

298 4.623

305 3.556

304 1.468

302 1.142

300 1.668

273 4.591

276 2.945

258 .383

259 .472

264 .448

303 .707

Railway Inn

271 .395

272 .978

275 3.507

266 .670

265 .357

267 .440

270 .807

S.P

S.P

M.P

S.P

S.B

S.P

268 1.287

274 4.668

277 2.825

261 .415

260 .474

262 .490

269 .011

242 .890

241 1.552

243 .946

1.003

2.352

1.601

2.106

F.P 3.180

F.P.

230

231

IX.II.

232

233

234

.hed by the Director General at the Ordnance Survey Office, Southampton, 1903.

75

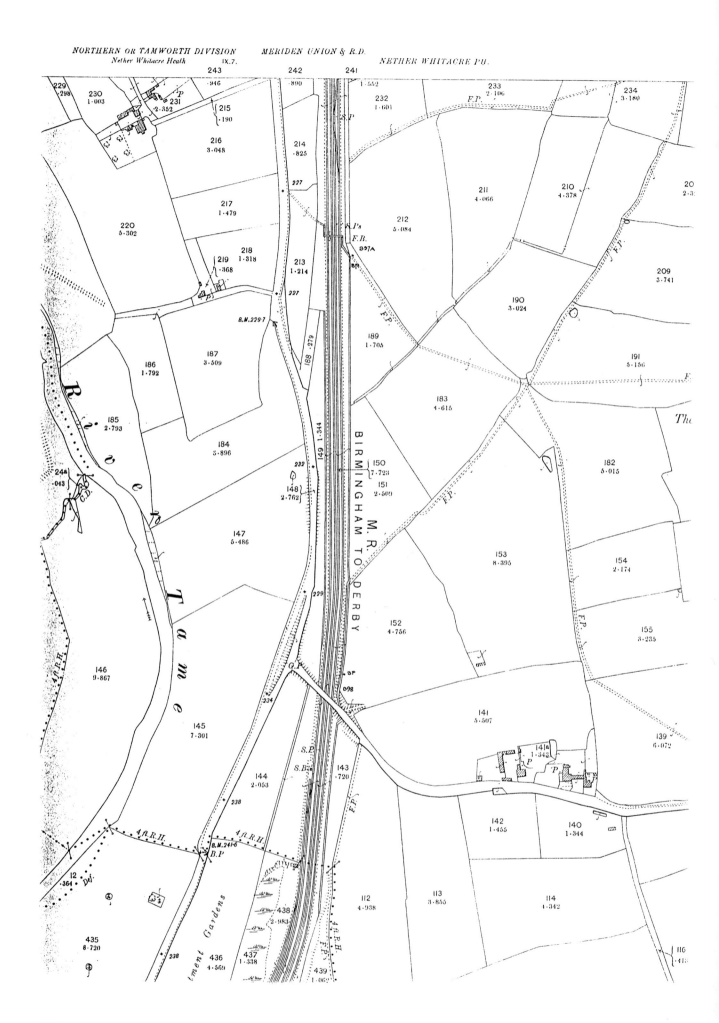

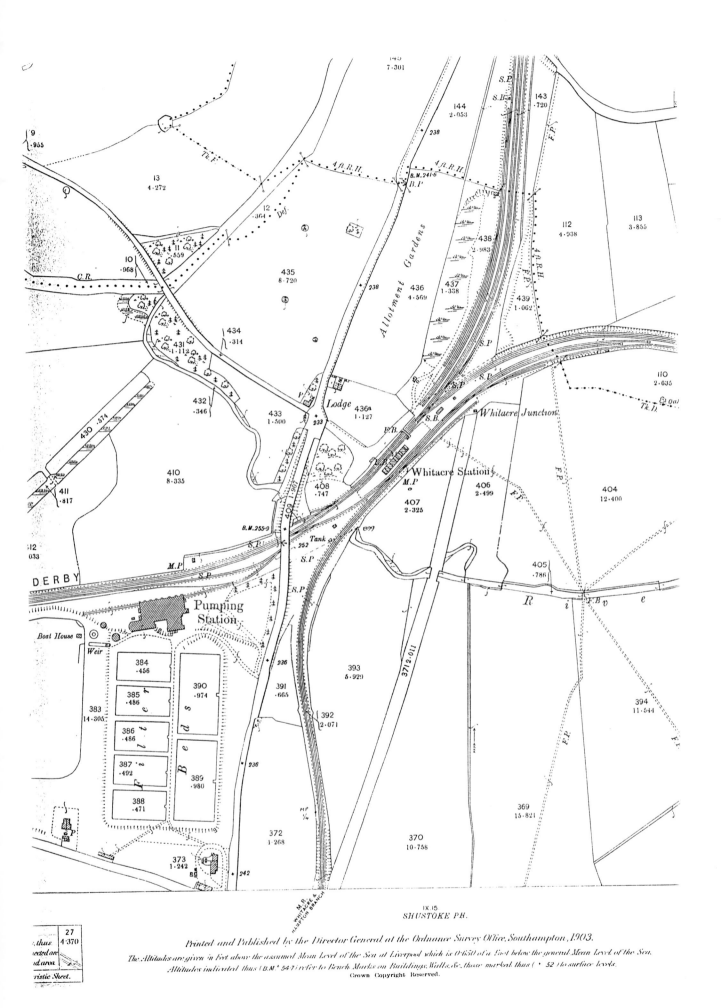

IX.15
SHUSTOKE P.H.

77

Samuel Waite Johnson. Chief engineer for the Midland Railway upon the death of Matthew Kirtley. His locomotives were to run on The Stonebridge Railway until its closure.

National Railway Museum

Class 8F Nº 48619 heads a coal train from Leicester through Whitacre Junction. Bound for Hams Hall, it nears the end of its journey.
R J Buckley

An unidentified Johnson 0-6-0 manfully hauls a heavy freight train from Derby past Whitacre Junction, c.1960.
Warwick County Record Office

Three views of Whitacre taken on 8 March 1956.

Towards Derby, the water tank alongside the down line can be seen.

Towards Birmingham.

Whitacre Junction signal box.   R M Casserley

Whitacre Station c.1960. The station was closed on 3 March 1968.

Courtesy RCHM

80

The view South of Whitacre station in the 1960s. The water tank at the commencement of the Hampton branch is on the left.

M J Lewis

Four views of Whitacre station in the early 1960s. Top right: *The old timber waiting room;* centre right: *Bikes at the rear;* bottom right: *Is that what was meant by the notice above? A Morris Minor takes advantage;* below: *The lamp at the station entrance.*

M J Lewis

Whitacre Junction c.1956. The original B&DJR track bed can be seen to the right of the picture.

Courtesy M J Lewis

The view south from Bridge No. 1. Photo taken 8 August 1916. The Whitacre distant signal is seen just beyond the Coleshill Road Bridge.

Courtesy R S Carpenter

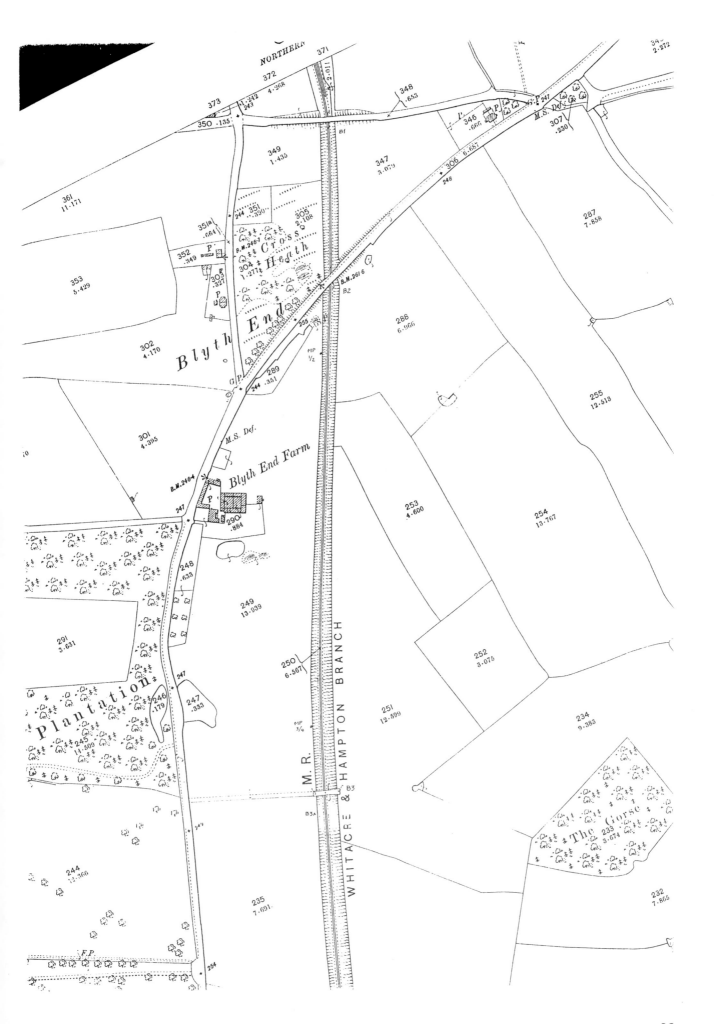

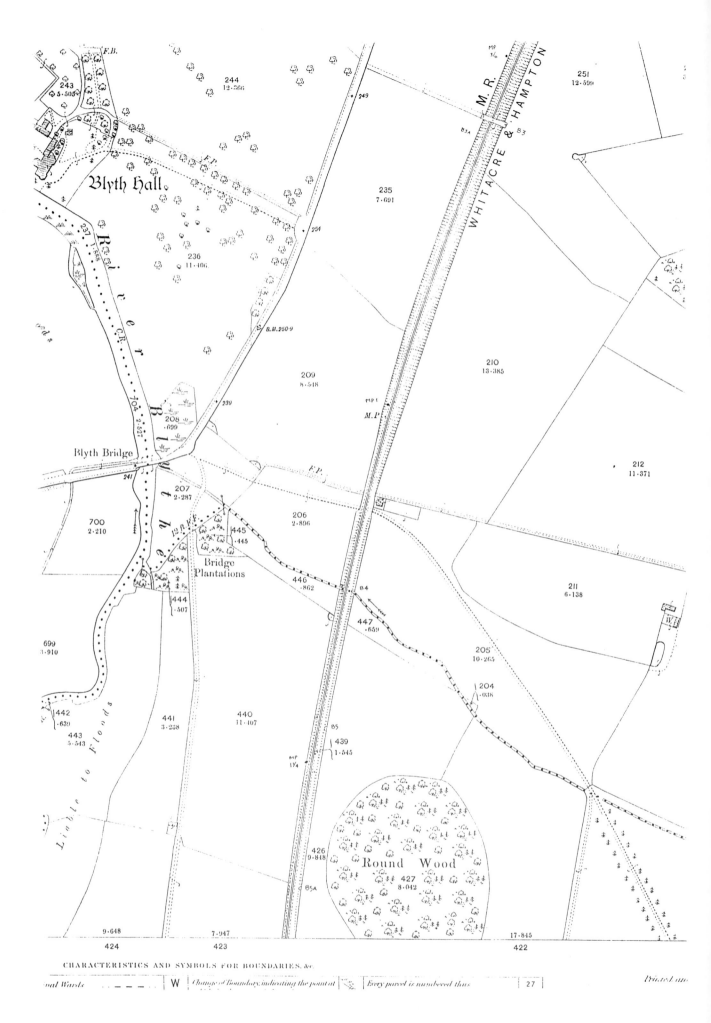

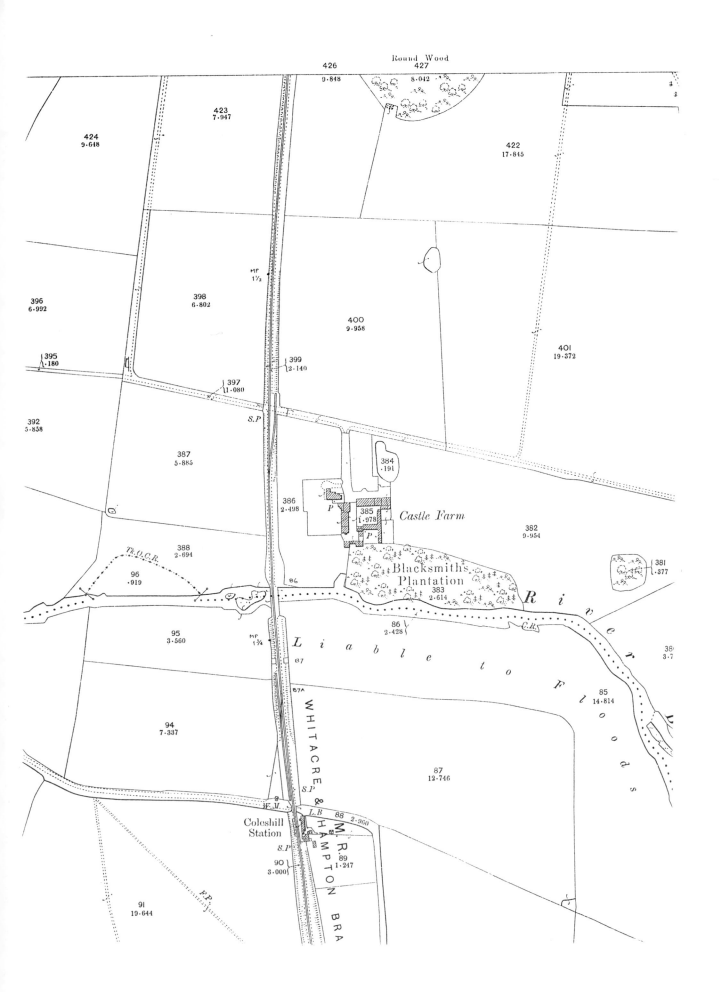

Round Wood

426
9·848

427
8·042

423
7·947

424
9·648

422
17·845

396
6·992

398
6·802

400
9·958

401
19·372

MP
1½

395
·180

399
2·140

397
1·080

392
5·858

S.P

387
5·885

384
·191

386
2·498

385
1·978

Castle Farm

382
9·954

381
·377

388
2·694

Tk.O.C.R.

96
·919

Blacksmiths
Plantation

383
2·614

R   i   v   e   r

95
3·560

MP
1¼

B6

86
2·428

C.R.

86

L   i   a   b   l   e   t   o

38
3·7

85
14·814

F   l   o   o   d   s

94
7·337

B7

B7A

87
12·746

WHITACRE &

S.P

W.M.

L.B

88
2·960

Coleshill
Station

S.P

M.   R.   HAMPTON   BRA

90
3·000

89
1·247

91
19·644

F.P

85

Bridge 6 at Castle Farm c.1963. The piers supporting the double track line still breast the currents today.

T H Messenger

Maxstoke station c.1951. The crossing gates have gone, but the house was in use up to 1962.

National Railway Museum

Coleshill station 1920. Viewed from Bridge 8, one of Rollason's box vans is in the siding.

Courtesy R S Carpenter

The view towards Coleshill Station in 1920. Coleshill home signal is in the background, and the cable for the distant signal is seen on the left.

Courtesy R S Carpenter

The view south from Bridge 8 towards river bridge 9. The Coleshill distant signal is just visible beyond the bridge. Photo dated 24 September 1920.

Courtesy R S Carpenter

Bridge 9 across the Blythe at Coleshill in 1920. The station was to the left.

Courtesy R S Carpenter

The Stonebridge Railway. The sidings remain, though. It is here in 1983 that the Prince of Wales requested the workmen in the depot opposite to move away because of their disturbances! In 1976 his father had not been so brusque.

The branch line water tank is shown on the map, together with the position of signals, as we approach MP 1/4. A gas processing plant now occupies the old curved approach to Whitacre station. Beneath our feet is bridge 1B, a 20" diameter cast iron pipe laid in a subway. On the 1839 track bed we see the brick built bridge over the River Bourne, and the raised nature of the ground is well in evidence. At Bridge 1 the two tracks meet.

Whitacre Junction to Maxstoke Lodge.

The large three-arch brick bridge on Shustoke Road was filled in long ago, but the view from it to the north is useful. A green strip indicates the very old route. To the south is Cross Heath, and small trees cover the ground. Bridge 2 spans the busy Coleshill Road. When built it had a single skew arch. Just beyond it in private land is the base of the Whitacre approach signal, and the post of MP 1/2. We now enter the deep and sheltered cutting once favoured by royalty. Imagine if you can a young lad creeping down the steeply wooded bank, up to a window of one of the gleaming coaches, and slipping away undetected with the Royal Soap! Did the future King Edward VIII really stroll out of the undergrowth to pass the time of day with Harry Clarke, the horse breeder? What tales that milepost could tell. Today the ground is a dense elongated wood. Steps appear in the bankside behind Blyth End Farm, and a few sleepers are found underfoot. The sole surviving milepost found in original, erect, and complete condition comes from this cutting. MP 3/4 has been lovingly restored and will one day find an appropriate home.

We tread carefully until eventually Bridge 3 comes into view, and we admire a fine example of the elliptical brick arch used so often on the line. Having a single 30ft. span, with a rise of 8' 11", it stands in excellent repair. Beneath its arch can be seen the remains of sleepers undisturbed by the elements thanks to its protecting cover. The ivy-clad parapets give the impression of having been like that since time immemorial. Immediately following is bridge 3A, a 12" culvert at surface level. Its brick channel rises strongly up the west face of the embankment. The track bed eases a little to MP 1, whose post is prominent. We reach a fence bordering a public footpath that crosses the line at right angles. Here is the ornate lodge erected at the entrance to Maxstoke Estate, and today it continues to provide idyllic accommodation.

Maxstoke Lodge to Coleshill Station.

At the end of the private garden that now occupies the track, the line rises to be carried across agricultural land by a low embankment. Here is bridge 4 – a large culvert taking a stream. Just before MP 1 1/4 another, smaller culvert, bridge 5, passes beneath. MP 1 1/4 was discovered lying horizontally in thick bracken. It too has been restored, and stands outside the author's house for all to see. Opposite Round Wood, in dense undergrowth, we pass bridge 5A, a 14" pipe with a stone flag top at its outlet. Sleepers still adorn the track in places. A farm crossing precedes the post of MP 1 1/2. No ammunition trains now for Eric Miller and Coleshill Fire Service to worry about.

A well-trodden footpath from Coleshill to Shustoke crosses the line on the level at the site of Maxstoke sidings. Here was where the ARP had to deal with Mustard Gas and the wrecked points. Here too was the Coleshill distant signal, near to the gatepost. The private road that passes Castle Farm follows exactly the old line, and it is difficult not to feel a sense of awe when looking down it. One can easily imagine the young Victoria's royal train approaching, with all the loyal estate workers cheering its progress. The substantial iron girder bridge No. 6 carries the road over the River Blythe, and its stone piers continue to battle against the currents. For a time a water tank was sited alongside this bridge. Within a few yards is the position of the now absent MP 1 3/4, and then the small, but neat iron girder overbridge, No. 7, beneath which the cattle got stuck in the mud. Bridge 7A, a culvert is next, and then we approach the site of Rollason's coal wharf on the west side of the line.

The yard adjoined Maxstoke Lane, and the triangular plot it occupied is still easily discernible, as is its concrete perimeter. When the timber bridges were demolished it was Phil Rollason who bartered coal for the steam cranes as exchange for the tubing from the bridge parapets. At the level crossing now reached it was he that had to wait patiently for the Beyer-Garratt to extricate its load of 180 crippled wagons. Here too, the gates at which Frankie Neale allowed at least one driver to take his train through without bothering to open them first!

Across the lane we enter a semi-private copse that takes us past the site of Coleshill Station down to the river. Little can be seen now of Bill Leary's home, and the undergrowth hides all but the barest remains of its footings. Long gone are the times when he would beg coal from a passing engine, or the very special day when his

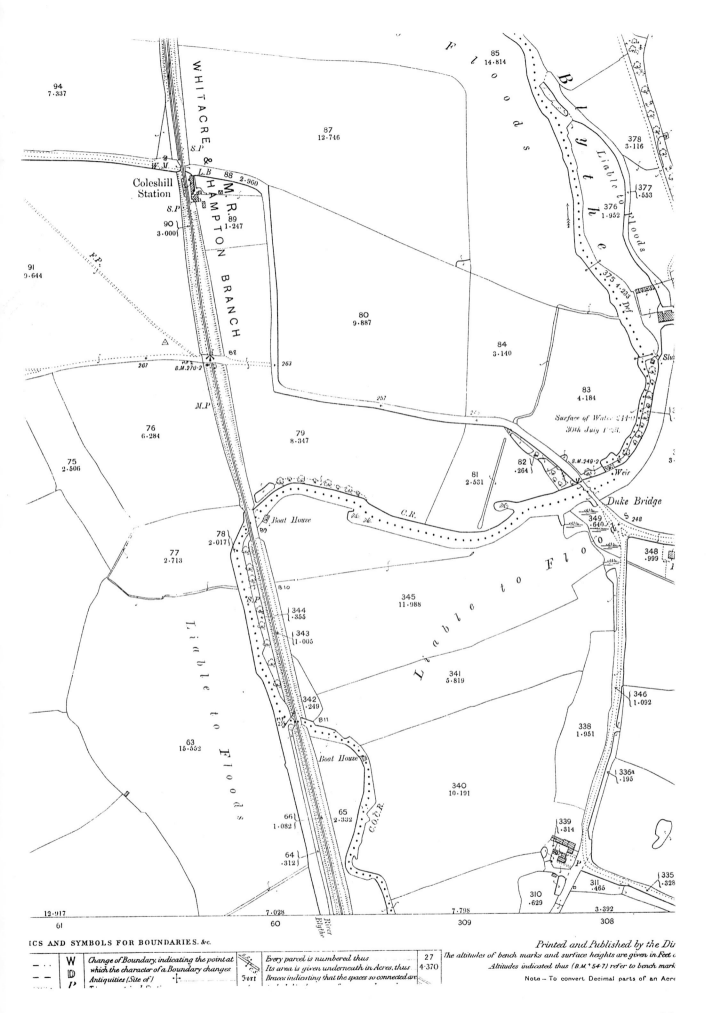

94
7·337

WHITACRE & HAMPTON BRANCH

87
12·746

85
14·814

Floods

Blythe

Liable to Floods

378
3·116

377
·553

376
1·952

S.P
W.M
L.B

Coleshill
Station

88 2·960

S.P

90
3·000

89
1·247

375 4·233 Def

91
9·644

F.P

80
9·887

84
3·140

M.P

267
B.M.270·2

263

83
4·184

Slu

257

Surface of Water ... H...
30th July 1...

82
·264

B.M.249·2

Weir

76
6·284

79
8·347

81
2·531

Duke Bridge

349
·640

S 248

75
2·506

Boat House

C.R.

348
·999

Liable to Flo

77
2·713

78
2·017

B10

345
11·988

346
1·092

344
·355

343
1·005

341
5·819

338
1·951

Liable to Floods

63
15·552

342
·249

B11

Boat House

340
10·191

336ª
·195

66
1·082

65
2·332

C.O.C.R.

339
·314

335
·328

64
·312

311
·465

310
·629

308

12·917

61

7·028

60

River Blythe

7·798

309

3·392

Printed and Published by the Dū

ICS AND SYMBOLS FOR BOUNDARIES. &c.

W	Change of Boundary, indicating the point at which the character of a Boundary changes	Every parcel is numbered thus	27
D	Antiquities (Site of)	Its area is given underneath in Acres, thus	4·370
P		Braces indicating that the spaces so connected are	Fort

the altitudes of bench marks and surface heights are given in Feet ...

Altitudes indicated thus (B.M. 54·7) refer to bench mark...

Note – To convert Decimal parts of an Acre...

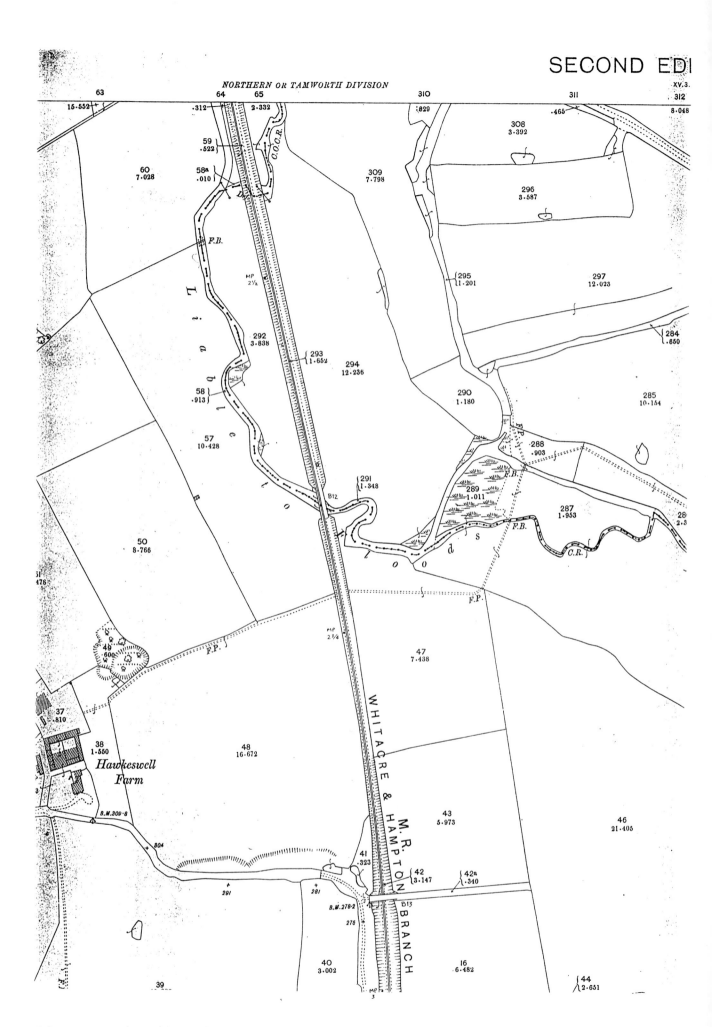

The remains of Bridge 9 in 1951, as viewed from the northern abutments.

Bridge 12 c.1951. The remnants of the timber supports make a sombre sight.

widow was presented with five bags of coal to mark her 100th birthday. No more mis-directed goods for him to take to Forge Mills station in his pony and trap. Can we hear the local bobby, surprising Mr. Whittaker (up on the roof with hammer poised), and asking what he was doing? "Removing the lead from this roof, officer". Was our blue-coated friend a bit nervous at that unexpected admission? "Oh, yes, and by whose authority, might I ask?" he persisted, unwisely. "By the authority in this letter" came the crushing reply from the roof, followed by a slip of paper with its prominent 'British Rail' heading. Perhaps we can share his hurried, red-faced exit from the bushes in which he had been hiding so optimistically.

Coleshill Station to Hawkeswell.

The dense bracken leads us past the base of an old platelayer's hut to Bridge 8, a handsome example of a skew arch that made extensive use of the local sandstone. Although a little vandalised now, it still impresses. It carries a public footpath overhead. Almost touching its south column we find MP 2, alas, like all the other remaining posts, minus its pediment. We stand on the brick abutments of bridge 9 to survey the bend in the river below, and note the stubs of the timber supports just visible beneath the surface of the stream. How many roach and chub have been caught here by relaxing railwaymen? No sign today of the old boat house opposite.

Through a pleasantly wooded stretch the raised line continues on its way to bridge 10, a 2' 6" culvert that takes a brook under our feet. We see on our right the brick remains of the base of the Coleshill distant signal, and then at bridge 11 a stockade of old sleepers surround the entrance to a dried up arm of the river. MP 2 1/4 was actually on this bridge. From here we can see the straight line taken by the Blythe on our right as a result of its diversion.

Some rough shooting ground now occupies the track bed at MP 2 1/2, and after passing the remains of another platelayer's hut the line opens out to bridge 12, another favourite fishing haunt. The timber supports of the bridge still provide snags for the unwary! A short cinder path extends from the other side, where a public footpath crosses over. MP 2 3/4 is found a few yards further on. From level ground a cutting develops, and bridge 13 stands serenely amongst the quiet farmland. Containing 3 ivy-covered spans, it carries a farm track over our heads.

Hawkeswell to Packington Ford.

The undergrowth gets thicker as we pass by the site of MP 3, and the thunder of traffic from the M6 destroys all sense of tranquillity. Beneath the motorway was an old farm crossing, and bridge 14. Both were lost in the re-routing of the river necessary for the road's construction, but the bridge abutments can still be picked out from the remains of the embankment to the south. Across picturesque arable farmland the line proceeds on top of a prominent embankment to MP 3 1/4, and then to a small girder bridge, No. 15, built to cross a well-established public right of way. Remnants of an older bridge can be seen in the brick footings.

Before long the sight of what is left of bridge 16 presents itself. This is the one that caused the severance of the line in 1935 following a severe weakening of its structure. The resident trout swim happily amongst its rotting piles, sharing the waters with large chub and greedy gudgeon. Across the other side we pick our way over the bricks and through thickets to see the post of MP 3 1/2. From there a tree-lined path through the woodlands of Todd's Rough marks the route. MP 3 3/4 denotes our emergence, and the line runs on the level across a small waterway where once lay a culvert, bridge 16A, of which only a few bricks now remain.

Into a cutting we near Packington Lane, with the crumbling remains of the wartime concrete loading platform on our right. Bridge 17 looms overhead, again resplendent in ivy. The parapets are somewhat battered, but its future is assured as a means of access to the ford and Packington Estate.

Packington Ford to Chester Road.

Brook Farm hovers above us in the damp and muddy depths of the cutting towards MP 4. It was here that the first line surveyed was to make its turn across Packington Park. The seventh Earl of Aylesford prevented that, but his descendants made good use of the railway, nevertheless. The sight of the present Earl's grandfather scuttling along the line on a *lurry* to go fishing must have been quite alarming. Private ownership of such vehicles was frowned upon by the railway authorities, and there were some close calls when the anglers became too intent on their quarry. A quick heave-ho was needed to avoid a repetition of the Whitacre accident! Deep grasses and nettles now dictate the going. Occasionally some old sleepers can be felt underfoot.

The landfill site towers above the line to the west, and a methane gas extraction plant occupies the track bed ahead. Behind its pungent bricks once stood MP 4 1/4. In a short distance bridge 18 is in view, and once more the sight of masses of ivy take us back to a different age. This is where the photographer stood to

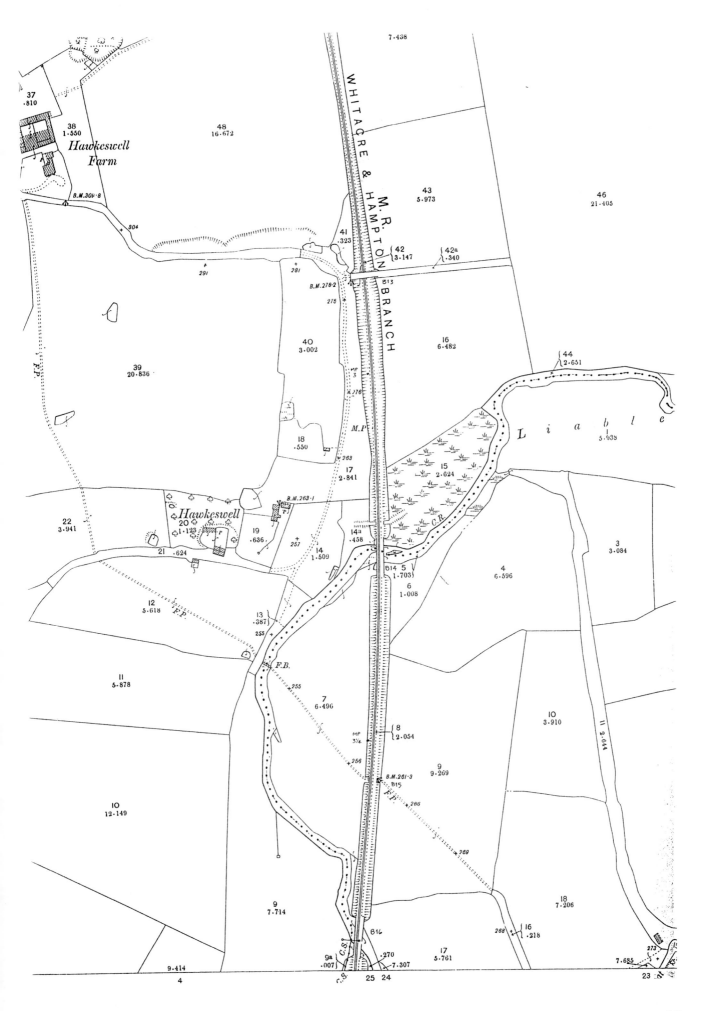

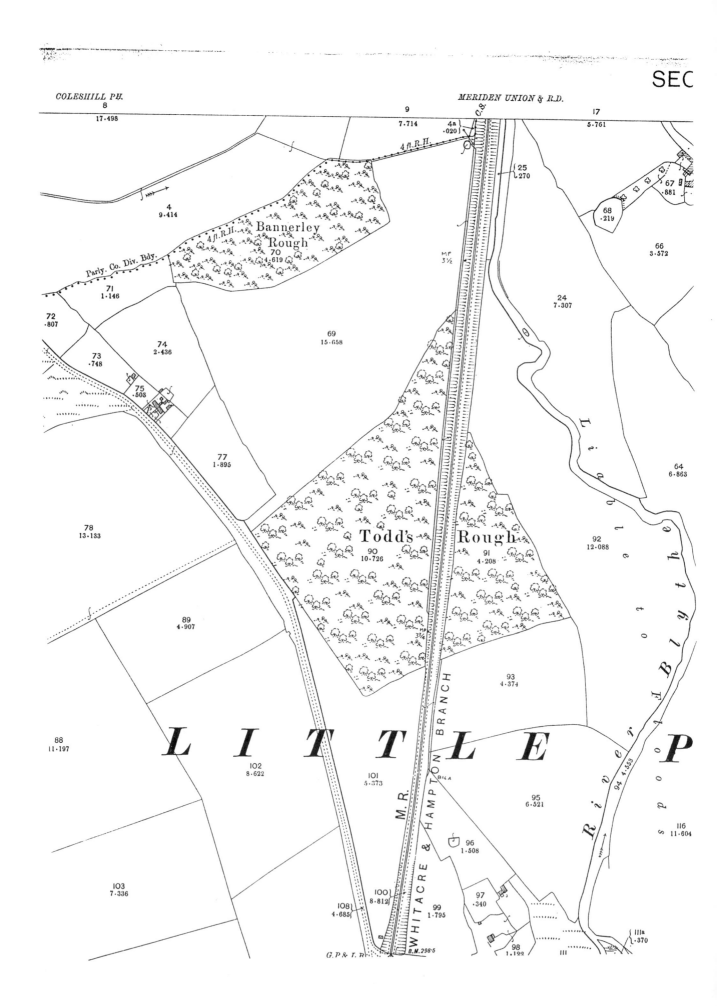

COLESHILL PH.
8
17·498

MERIDEN UNION & R.D.
9
7·714

17
5·761

4a
·020

4 fl. R.H.

25
·270

4 fl. R.H.

4
9·414

M.P
3½

Bannerley
Rough
70
4·619

67
·881

68
·219

66
3·572

Parly. Co. Div. Bdy.

71
1·146

24
7·307

72
·807

74
2·436

69
15·658

73
·748

75
·503

64
6·863

77
1·895

78
13·133

Todd's   Rough
90
10·726

91
4·208

92
12·088

89
4·907

93
4·374

88
11·197

L I T T L E   P

102
8·622

101
5·373

95
6·521

116
11·604

96
1·508

M.R.

WHITACRE & HAMPTON BRANCH

103
7·336

100
8·812

97
·340

108
4·685

99
1·795

111a
·370

98
1·122

111

G.P & T.R

B.M. 298·5

94
4·553

River Blythe   spoot

Bridge 13 in 1920. Facing Whitacre the line curves to the left as it passes Hawkeswell Farm.

Courtesy R S Carpenter

Bridge 21A, Packington Park in 1954. It never carried a train. Built as a substitute for an estate bridge lost during rerouting of the River Blythe, it was maintained by the railways up to 1947.

P J Garland collection. Courtesy R S Carpenter

MP 4¼ c.1951. Now the site of a gas processing plant.
Courtesy Lawrence Ellis

The line at Packington in 1920. A single coal wagon inhabits the siding.

Courtesy R S Carpenter

The line at MP 5 c.1951. The Chester Road Bridge had recently been filled in. The pediment of MP 5 now adorns a house in Balsall Common.

National Railway Museum

The line between the Coventry Road and the Chester Road in 1921. MP 5¼ can just be seen in the middle distance. Siding Wood is in the background. Viewed towards Coleshill from Bridge 24.

Courtesy R S Carpenter

A view of the line to the south of the Chester Road bridge, near MP 5. The track curves towards Bickenhill and the Coventry Road. Photo taken 1st April 1921.

Courtesy R S Carpenter

Looking towards Hampton from Bridge 25. The cutting is well in evidence here. Due to its depth and proximity to a stream it was often subject to flooding, so was filled in after closure. The public footpath runs along its east side. Another shot of the line on All Fools Day 1921.

Courtesy R S Carpenter

The cutting north of MP 5¾ in 1921. Bridge 24 can just be seen in the distance. Hampton distant signal is on the left. Viewed from Bridge 25 facing towards Whitacre, the cutting was filled in at closure.

Courtesy R S Carpenter

An unusual penance! On the line at Hampton c.1950.

Authors' collection

Hampton c.1950. The station was by then in use as a house.

Lens of Sutton

Bridge 27 – August 1963. One of the last engines on the branch, Class 8F 48723 crosses to the short section of siding north of Hampton.
Courtesy Dr. Alan Smyth

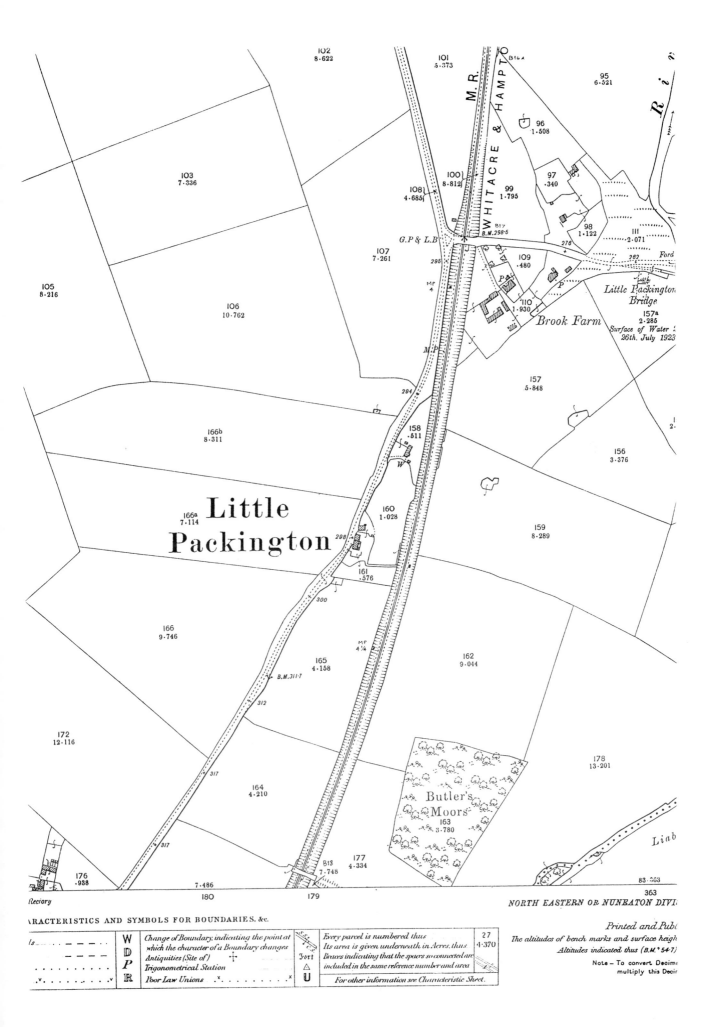

Little

Packington

Brook Farm

Little Packington Bridge

Butler's Moors

102
8·622

101
5·373

95
6·521

96
1·508

97
·340

99
1·795

100
8·812

108
4·685

98
1·122

111
2·071

103
7·336

107
7·261

109
·480

G.P & L.B

B.M.298·5

157ᵃ
2·285

Surface of Water
26th. July 1923

110
1·930

157
5·848

105
8·216

106
10·762

166ᵇ
8·311

158
·511

156
3·376

160
1·028

159
8·289

166ᵃ
7·114

161
·576

166
9·746

165
4·158

B.M.311·7

162
9·044

172
12·116

178
13·201

164
4·210

163
3·780

176
·938

177
4·334

Rectory

180

179

83·383

363

M.R.

WHITACRE & HAMPTO...

R i ...

NORTH EASTERN OR NUNEATON DIVI...

CHARACTERISTICS AND SYMBOLS FOR BOUNDARIES, &c.

Is........	W D P R	Change of Boundary, indicating the point at which the character of a Boundary changes	Every parcel is numbered thus
		Antiquities (Site of)	Its area is given underneath in Acres, thus
		Trigonometrical Station	Braces indicating that the spaces so connected are included in the same reference number and area
		Poor Law Unions	For other information see Characteristic Sheet.

27
4·370

Printed and Publi...

The altitudes of bench marks and surface heigh...

Altitudes indicated thus (B.M.ᵃ 54·7)...

Note – To convert Decim...
multiply this Decim...

101

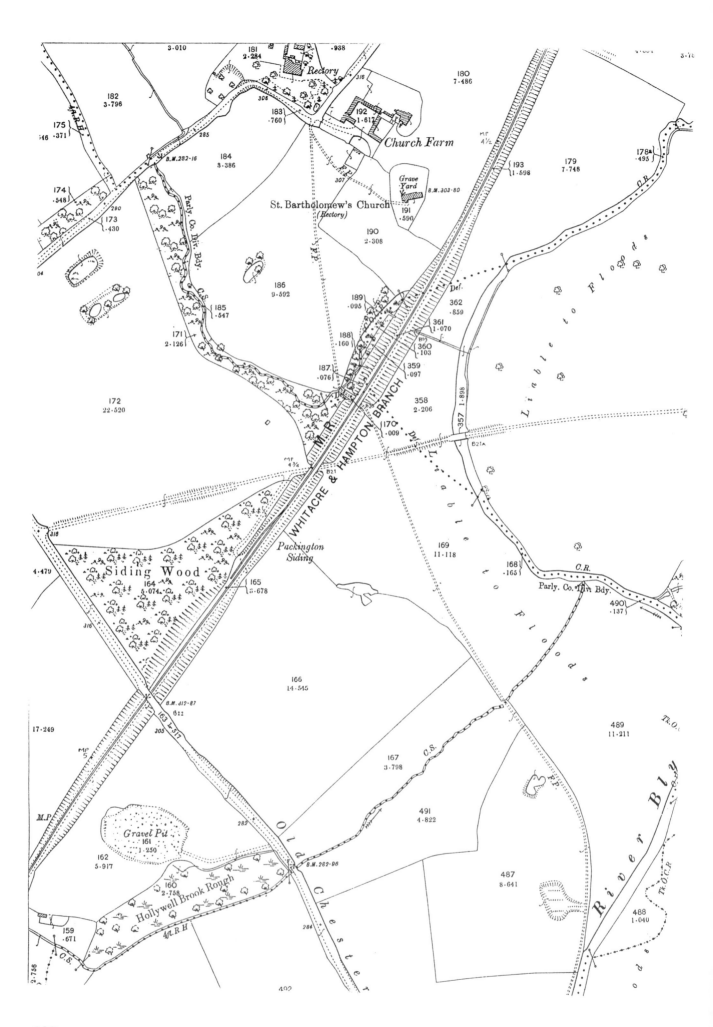

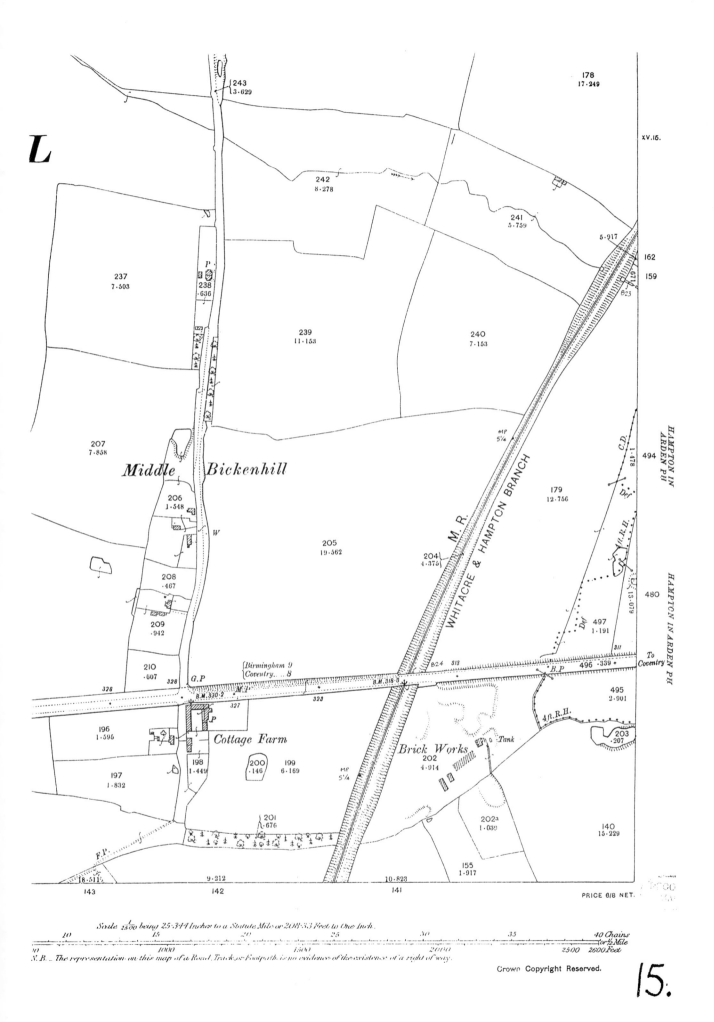

L

243
3·629

178
17·249

242
8·278

241
5·759

XV.15.

5·917

162
159
B23

237
7·503

P
238
·636

239
11·153

240
7·153

MP
5¼

HAMPTON IN ARDEN PH

C.D
1·478
Def
494

207
7·858

Middle   Bickenhill

W

206
1·548

205
19·562

M. R.

179
12·756

4ft.R.H
13·079
480

HAMPTON IN ARDEN PH

208
·467

204
4·375

WHITACRE & HAMPTON BRANCH

Def
497
1·191

209
·942

210
·607

G.P
328

Birmingham 9
Coventry . 8

M.P

B24   313

311
To
Coventry

328

B.M.330·2

B.M.318·0

323

B.P
496 ·339

495
2·901

4ft.R.H

327

196
1·595

P

Cottage Farm

200
·146

199
6·169

Brick Works
202
4·914

Tank

203
·207

198
1·449

197
1·832

MP
5¼

202a
1·039

140
15·229

201
·676

F.P.

155
1·917

18·511

9·212

10·823

143

142

141

PRICE 6/8 NET.

15.

103

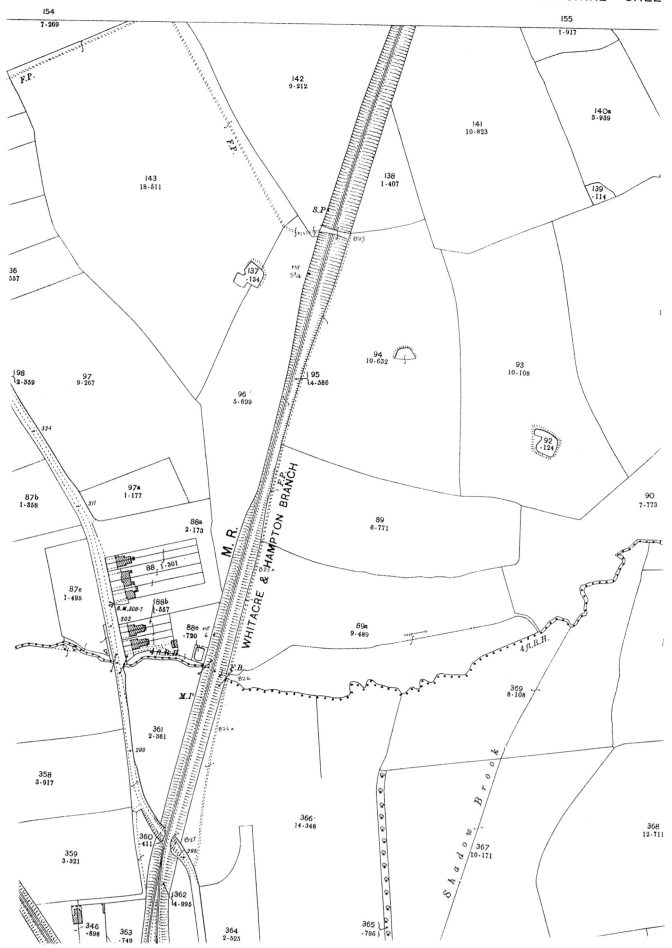

obtain his wonderfully evocative shot of the daily Hampton – Whitacre train. Under its ample arch, the track beneath deteriorates once more as nature takes over. As we reach MP 4 1/2 St. Bartholomew's Church is on our right. Closed now, vandals have left their mark upon it, although private ownership offers hope.

A tree-lined stream trickles by far below us in *The Bell* as the line enters Packington Park upon a high embankment. Three bridges now follow in the space of 200 yards. Below us a substantial culvert, bridge 19, takes the water from a stream. This is where the River Blythe was diverted, but the Parish Boundary follows its former route. Bridge 20 is a lovely 3 arch viaduct of sandstone and brick. The ever-present ivy hides much of its form, but good views can be had from the right of way below.

Whilst at this point, bridge 21A is easily seen across the fields. This ostentatious farm crossing was built by the B&DJR and maintained by a succession of railway companies until as late as 1947. It is of an unnecessarily elaborate design, with stone piers and a small arch having stone voussirs. A few yards further on is bridge 21, upon which once stood MP 4 3/4. Another classic example of a skew arch, this is a magnificent bridge. Again though, the ubiquitous ivy has claimed it as its own.

On our right here is the start of Packington Siding, from which the wood above took its name. Remnants of the points are scattered upon the ground, but the old oak beam of the stop block appears indestructible. The cutting below Siding Wood is thickly populated by thorn bushes, and it is a relief to reach Bridge 22. This carried the Chester Road. Although now filled in, the bridge was of a workmanlike square form, though still making sensible and attractive use of local materials.

Chester Road to Hampton.

Upon crossing the highway we are again consigned into bracken. MP 5 still stands, minus its pediment. The daughter of Len Reeves, the Hampton stationmaster, has this particular relic standing proudly outside her house, at No. 5 of course, and most appropriately decorated with ivy. The line curves slightly south now as we approach Bridge 23, a sizeable culvert that carries Hollywell Brook. By the time we arrive at MP 5 1/4, trees are again enclosing our passage. A Hampton GP, whose weakness for railway artefacts was well known to his patients, secured milepost pediments 1/2, 1, and 5 1/4 to add to his considerable collection.

From this point on the track all evidence of past civilisation disappears. We look for a replica of the Chester Road bridge, but are disappointed. Road works surrounding the National Exhibition Centre dominate, although the bridge that now carries the Coventry Road across the line of the railway has at least retained some of the original stones in its parapets. This is bridge 24. Do not be fooled by a painted number 23 upon its north-east edge. As the road surface beneath emerges in a spiral, the line of the old railway proceeds straight ahead. MP 5 1/2 has been lost as a result of the access road. The level becomes considerably higher now. First, the road embankments are seen in front. Then follows a fenced off section.

Here was a deep cutting on the approaches to Hampton. Frequently subject to flooding, it was filled and now permits access to and from the adjacent sand pits. Today it is home to countless rabbits. The wide surface soon reaches a public footpath leading from the rear of the National Motorcycle Museum. Where this path meets the line, bridge 25 stood. Almost identical to bridge 18, its rubble now lies buried beneath our feet. No more a hiding place for Tonks the platelayer to fall asleep in his hut, only to have a young W.D.Butler throwing stones at his door! Not even a place in which to retire beneath his upturned barrow for a quick nap. Happy days! The Hampton distant signal has disappeared too. Perhaps though, MP 5 3/4 is intact beneath the stony surface?

The footpath continues southwards, parallel to the line, and on its eastern side. We can see clearly the return of the track to its former levels, and the scene is once again reminiscent of grander days. Amongst the track side heather lie piles of old sleepers left in 1952. Do we hear the sound of Driver Jack Hancox's engine as it pushes the steam crane in? Or the warnings of his fireman Arthur Smith to avoid the overhanging branches that had almost dragged a guard from a previous train? Perhaps. We cross over a small brick barrel pipe, bridge 25A, before finding ourselves alongside an old piece of rail embedded in concrete, and covered in ivy. Lying deep in the undergrowth, it represents all that is left of MP 6. To carry a large brook, a well-preserved brick culvert can be observed from the footpath below. This is bridge 26. Another smaller one, bridge 26A, follows.

The path of the line falls away approaching Old Station Road, and the concrete foundations of the secret Air Ministry Base are seen all around. Even an old gate survives where bridge 27 once stood. The bend in the road here made life difficult for traffic, and so the bridge had to go. It was of solid stone and brick construction, just like all the others, and it wasn't going to fall down by itself.

Material recovery train at Hampton in 1951.

Contractor's crane on line in 1951.

Courtesy Lawrence Ellis

Contractor's crane on line in 1951.

Contractor's loco at Hampton in 1951.

Courtesy Lawrence Ellis

Material recovery train at Hampton in 1951.

Courtesy Lawrence Ellis

Hampton signal frame in 1951, all that was left of the old Midland box at the junction. Opposite is the LMS signal box that took over control of the branch.

Courtesy Lawrence Ellis

The last train to run on the branch proper. Driver Jack Hancox and fireman Arthur Smith on the footplate of Ivatt class 6P No. 46446 in 1951.

Courtesy Lawrence Ellis

Black Five No. 45058 hauls a dismantling train at Hampton in February 1965

Courtesy Dr. Alan Smyth

Alfred and Harriet Lee c.1920. Last stationmaster at Hampton Midland.

Courtesy Dr. J W Bland

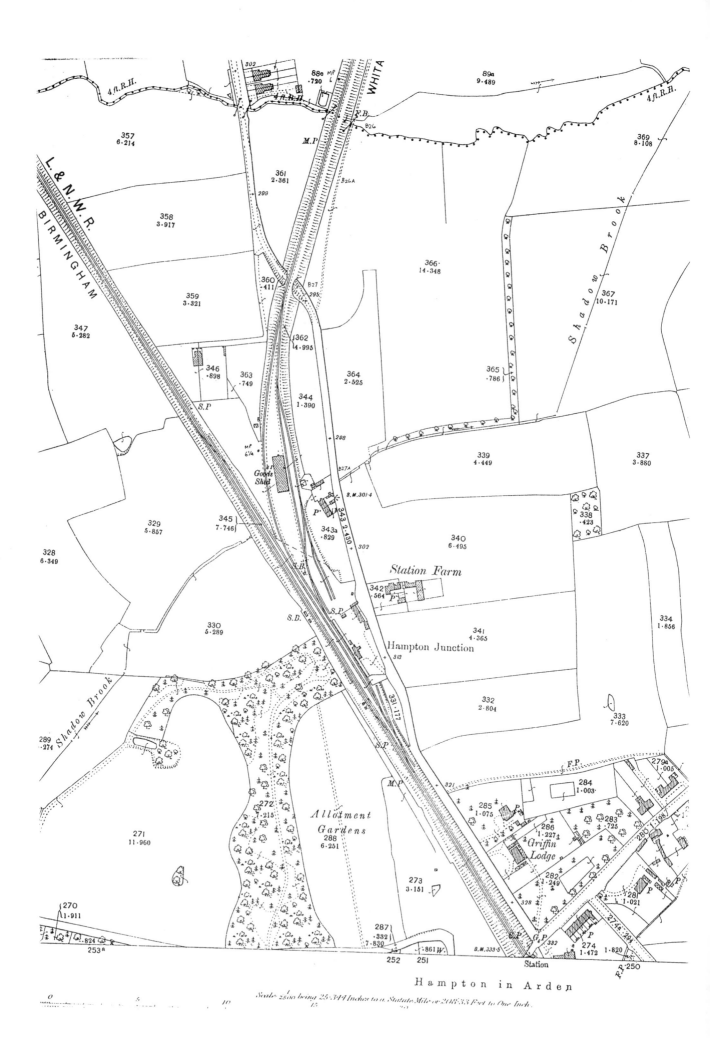

Hampton.

Down a track leading off The Grove can be found Vale House, the home of Allport and Kirtley. The best view of it can be had from a train on the adjacent main line. At the bend in the road, right on top of the old line can be found a much newer residence. Just before fields on the left of the road as we approach Station Farm, a brick culvert passes beneath the road and the railway. This bridge, 27A, is the last.

The yards of Wyckham Blackwell now dominate the scene. The workshops represent the site of the old engine shed, and indeed one wall of it survives. The fire of 1977 destroyed the rest. MP 6 1/4, the final one, stood level with the rear of the building. A short, broken post was recently discovered by the author at the side of the line near to bridge 26, and it is probably this very one. Next to a gate can be observed an old office, adjacent to which is the Midland Railway weighbridge, still intact.

Beyond lies the station of 1839. Consisting of a main booking hall and associated waiting rooms, it has an adjoining parcels office. Its last stationmaster, Mr. Lee, looked after it well. Its future was assured in 1992 with the granting of a Grade II listing, and since then the station site has been carefully and sympathetically restored by its owners. The platform, though now much reduced in length, is the same one that so many royal visitors have graced.

So we come to the end of our journey. Hampton station holds many happy memories for the author. In particular, the parcels office. This book was written in it.

Recommended further reading

The Birmingham and Derby Junction Railway by Charles Clinker. A masterly account in the form of a short paper to the Dugdale Society.

The Midland Counties Railway by the Derby Railway History Research Group. A most detailed record of that railway's development, with useful background information about other schemes and companies.

The Midland Railway by C.H.Ellis. An excellent all-round account.

The Midland Railway: A Narrative of Modern Enterprise by F.S.Williams. Written in the mid 19th Century, it presents a superb account of the workings of the company. Together with *Our Iron Roads* by the same author they are the seminal works from one of the earliest railway historians.

The Rise of the Midland Railway by E.G.Barnes. A noted reference work with some good illustrations.

A Regional History of the Railways of Great Britain, Volume 7; and Forgotten Railways by Rex Christiansen. Two brief overviews of the line's history.

Railway Locomotive Management – The Letters of Veritas Vincit. Exceptionally detailed and often amusing insights into the early workings of railways.

British Railway Journal No 5 – Autumn 1984. R.S. Carpenter's informative and fine pictorial account of the branch.

Railway Magazine – November 1963 and January 1964. A brief but atmospheric look at the line by T.H. Messenger, and a subsequent letter.

Railway Magazine – March and June 1950. A short but neat article by Eric S. Tonks, followed by further correspondence.

The Railway and Travel Monthly – Vol. XI 1915. Contains a detailed look at "Railways in Warwickshire".

Railway Magazine – 1902. Includes an often overlooked item entitled "The Railways of Warwickshire" that has great period charm.

Reference sources

Acts of Parliament related to the Birmingham and Derby Junction Railway.
Board and Traffic minutes of the Birmingham and Derby Junction Railway.
The diaries of Queen Victoria.
The Midland Railway – A Chronology, by John Gough.
Railways of the West Midlands – A Chronology.
Trading in Timber by W.D.Butler.
Illustrated London News.
Aris' Birmingham Gazette.
The Birmingham Evening Mail.
The Coventry Evening Telegraph.
The Derbyshire Courier.
The Coleshill Chronicle.
The Locomotive magazine.
Railway Magazine.
Herepath's Journal.
Accident records at the National Railway Museum.
1916 Midland Railway Distance Diagrams.
1903/4 Ordnance Survey 25" series maps.
1841 Census returns.

Acknowledgements

The author wishes to express his grateful appreciation to the many people and organisations that have assisted in the preparation of this book. Invariably this help was given in a friendly and efficient manner, and services were rendered with the utmost professionalism.

For their kind permission in granting access to property and family archives, the writer is especially indebted to Lord Aylesford, Lord Guernsey, Sir William Stratford Dugdale, Captain C.B. Fetherston-Dilke, Mr. Michael Fetherston-Dilke, Mr. Nick Barlow, Mr. Marcus Finn, Mr. W.D. Butler, and Mr. Richard Bouverat. Special thanks too, to Robin Hurley; Conservation Architect to Solihull Metropolitan Borough Council, and John Yates; Inspector to English Heritage, for the Grade II listing of Hampton station. For their support in this respect Iain Mills, MP; The Hampton Society; Hampton-in-Arden Parish Council; The Fentham Trust; Coleshill Civic Society.

For archive material and photographs thanks to the following organisations and individuals: The Public Record Office, Kew. The County Record Offices, Warwick and Matlock. The Victoria and Albert Museum. The Royal Commission on the Historical Monuments of England. The British Library. British Rail London Midland Region. The National Railway Museum, York. The Institute of Civil Engineers. The Midland Railway Trust, Butterley. In particular J.C. Elliott, John Russell, M. Blakemore, C.P. Atkins, Carol Arrowsmith, and Dudley Foulkes. Pamela Clark at the Royal Archives, Windsor. Mark Higginson at the Derby Industrial Museum. Martin Ellis at the Birmingham Museums and Art Gallery. Personal thanks to the staff of libraries throughout the Midlands without whose knowledge and willing help little could have been achieved - notably those at Solihull Central Library, Birmingham Reference Library, and Derby Local Studies Library, as well as those at the smaller outposts at Chesterfield, Rugby, Coleshill, and Hampton.

Thanks are offered: For printed material, to: "Collectables" in Warwick. The Dugdale Society. The Branch Line Society. The Stephenson Locomotive Society. Haven Booksearch. Robert Humm & Co. The Locomotive Club of Great Britain. For photographic services, to: Geoffrey Creighton Studios, Rugby. Colin Brookes. Dr. J.W. Bland. For artefacts, to John Mander at the Birmingham Museum of Railwayana. For photographs, to: The Mary Evans Picture Library. Lens of Sutton. Dartmouth Museum. Wild Swan Publications. W.A. Camwell. R.M. Casserley. M.J. Lewis. Lawrence Ellis. Mike and Beryl Bryant. Peter Lee. Peter Butler. Margaret Lancaster. Mary Sutton. For his excellent booklet on research, to Peter Kay. For inspiration, to Roger S. Carpenter, whose article in British Railway Journal was a starting point, and whose photographic collection was so willingly put at the author's disposal. For much reference detail, to Brian Radford. For the loan of "The Letters of Veritas Vincit", to Dr. Tunbridge and Simon Davis. For the loan of artefacts and photographs, to Dr. Alan Smyth. For background history, to Anthony J. Bower. For traffic and time tables, to Geoffrey Hoyle and John Mills. For advice, to: Sue Bates. Michael Whitehouse. John Gough. Nick Howell. Bob Essory. Colin Gorton. For invaluable anecdotal contributions, to: Phil Rollason. Molly and Cyril Lane. Jim Locke. Charles Lines. Muriel Morris. Bill Mochrie. Tom Murdison. Oliver Suffield. Tom Wilcox. Eric Toone. Messrs. Peyton, Whittaker, Reading, and Powell. For interest shown, to: Ken Conway. John Shepherd. Colin Troth. John Miller. The late Eric Miller. For aid above and beyond the call of duty in rescuing iron relics, to John, Ted, Arthur and Alan Webb. Finally, for the onerous task of proof-reading the manuscript I am indebted to Janet Webb.

Index

BREWIN BOOKS

Transport and Military 1994–1995

ISBN	RAILWAYS			
0 947731 08 3	Steam on the Birmingham Gloucester Loop	Philip Jarvis	A5 (Landscape) Paperback	£6.40
0 947731 78 4	Cross City Connections (L.M.S.)	John Bassett	A4 Harback	£14.95
0 947731 89 X	The Lost Railways of Birmingham	Keith Turner	A5 Paperback	£5.95
1 85858 035 8	The Ross & Monmouth Railway	Mark Glover	A5 Paperback	£5.95
* 1 85858 045 5	The Stonebridge Railway	Roger Waring	A4 Hardback	£14.95
* 1 85858 034 X	The Harborne Express	R.J.M.Smith, C.D.Harrison	A5 Paperback	£5.95
	CANALS			
0 947731 49 0	Exploring the New River	Michael Essex-Lopresti	A5 Paperback	£6.95
0 947731 46 4	Building Britains Canals	David Gladwin	A5 (Landscape) Paperback	£6.95
1 85858 017 X	Exploring the Regents Canal	Michael Essex-Lopresti	A5 Paperback	£7.95
	ROAD TRANSPORT			
0 947731 71 1	Coaching Cavalcade – The British Motor Coach 1910–1970	David Gladwin	A4 Hardback	£14.95
0 947731 91 1	Midbus – Some Aspects of Midland Bus and Coach Operations	David Gladwin	A4 Hardback	£14.95
1 85858 013 7	Britain's Motor Buses – A Pictorial Review	David Gladwin	A5 (Landscape) Paperback	£8.95
1 85858 011 0	Vintage Style – The Story of Cross and Ellis	Gillian Bardsley	A4 Paperback	£8.95
1 85858 050 1	Monte-Carlo – The Mini Legend	(Ed) Trevor Lord	A4 Paperback	£11.95
1 85858 027 7	Sporting Volkswagens	Laurence Meredith	240×170mm Paperback	£10.95
1 85858 015 3	PSV Panorama	David Gladwin	A4 Hardback	£14.95
* 1 85858 038 2	Building Britains Tramways	David Gladwin	A5 (Landscape) Paperback	£8.95
* 1 85858 039 0	A Guide to Bus Preservation	John A Godwin	240×170mm Paperback	£10.95
	AVIATION HISTORY			
1 85858 020 X	Airship – The Story of R34	Patrick Abbott	240×170mm Paperback	£10.95

ISBN	Title	Author	Format	Price
1 85858 036 6	Aegean Masquerade (Covert R.A.F. Operations in W.W.II)	Stanley Beavan	A5 Paperback	£7.95
* 1 85858 054 4	Erk's Eye View (R.A.F. National Service)	Eric Russell	A5 Paperback	£7.95
* 1 85858 048 X	The Kipper Fleet (Sunderland Flying Boats)	Stanley Beavan	A5 Paperback	£7.95
* 1 85858 049 8	Building Britains Airships	Patrick Abbott	A5 (Landscape) Paperback	£8.95

POLICE & MILITARY HISTORY

ISBN	Title	Author	Format	Price
* 0 947731 18 8	From Rattle to Raio (London Metropolitan)	John Bunker	A5 Paperback	£9.95
0 947731 01 6	Policing Shropshire	Douglas Elliott	A5 Paperback	£5.40
0 947731 55 5	Policing Hereford & Leoominster	Gordon Forest, Ted Hadley	A4 Paperback	£10.95
0 947731 06 7	From Mons to Messines (W.W.I)	(Ed) Stephen Royle	A5 Paperback	£6.40
1 85858 016 1	Letters For Victory (W.W.II)	Martin & Frances Collins	240×170mm Paperback	£10.95

* NEW TITLES in preparation.

All orders and correspondence to:
BREWIN BOOKS: Doric House, 56 Alcester Road, Studley, Warwickshire, B80 7LG
Tel: 01527 854228   Fax: 01527 852746